BOA
EDITIONS
LIMITED

CRAZY HORSE IN STILLNESS

Poems

WILLIAM HEYEN

BOA Editions, Ltd.   ᗧ   Brockport, NY   ᗧ   1996

LC #: 95–77862
ISBN: 1–880238–28–4 cloth
ISBN: 1–880238–29–2 paper

First Edition
95 96 97 98   7 6 5 4 3 2 1

Publications by BOA Editions, Ltd.—
a not-for-profit corporation under section 501 (c) (3)
of the United States Internal Revenue Code—
are made possible with the assistance of grants from
the Literature Program of the New York State Council on the Arts,
the Literature Program of the National Endowment for the Arts,
the Lannan Foundation,
as well as from the Rochester Area Foundation Community Arts Fund
administered by the Arts & Cultural Council for Greater Rochester,
the County of Monroe, NY,
and from many individual supporters.

Cover Design: Daphne Poulin-Stofer
Art: "Victory Dance" (1954), by Oscar House,
Courtesy of the Philbrook Museum of Art, Tulsa, Oklahoma
Typesetting: Richard Foerster
Manufacturing: McNaughton & Gunn, Lithographers
BOA Logo: Mirko

BOA Editions, Ltd.
A. Poulin, Jr., President
92 Park Avenue
Brockport, NY 14420

I believe that when Crazy Horse was killed, something more than a man's life was snuffed out. Once, America's size in the imagination was limitless. After Europeans settled and changed it, working from the coasts inland, its size in the imagination shrank. Like the center of a dying fire, the Great Plains held that original vision longest. Just as people finally came to the Great Plains and changed them, so they came to where Crazy Horse lived and killed him. Crazy Horse had the misfortune to live in a place which existed both in reality and in the dreams of people far away; he managed to leave both the real and the imaginary place unbetrayed.

> Ian Frazier
> *Great Plains* (1989)

Our concept of time, which makes up part of our reason for being Indian, is that we have no concept of time.

> Russell Means
> Quoted in *The New York Times* (April 22, 1975)

Among the languages of American Indians there is no word for "art." For Indians everything is art . . . therefore it needs no name. My efforts, however, to find communicative accesses between the Native American world and the world of the dominant society convinced me that the metaphoric form of expression called "art" in the West is the best means of transcending the isolation of vastly dissimilar cultures. Curiously, this very important artistic connection can never be factual—for ultimately facts do not inform us. No matter how well informed a spectator may be on the techniques of the arts or the many aspects of an alien culture, if someone does not experience an aesthetic relationship to what is before him or her, all the information and education will not permit that person to cross the distance that exists between different peoples and, for that matter, between different individuals of the same technological society.
Art puts us in touch with "the other." Without art we are alone.

> Jamake Highwater
> *The Primal Mind: Vision and Reality in Indian America* (1981)

Custer's orders from Terry gave him considerable latitude. They outlined the route he was to take but contained the phrase: "It is, of course, impossible to give you any definite instructions in regard to this movement...." Also contained in the orders were the actions Custer was to take and the stipulation that Custer conform to those actions "...unless you see sufficient reason for departing from them."

> Bill and Jan Moeller
> *Custer: His Life, His Adventures* (1988)

The burden of the past that weighs like a nightmare on the brain of the west is an imperial burden, the anxiety that it might not all be of one piece, that secret histories, forgotten facts, other imaginations operate in all that we do and make, and that our massive ignorance of Othernesses is working to undermine what we do. Like Napoleon moving inexorably towards the capture of Moscow, Great Traditions follow their difficult and equivocal victories of imagination to an ultimate destruction.

> Jerome McGann
> "The Third World of Criticism" (1989)

What we feel in this history is a timeless, inexorable, trans-spatial, backfolding, lyric progression to the Battle of Little Bighorn.

> Edwina Seaver
> *1876 and All That* (1976)

I was in the power. I heard my long-dead relatives talking to me. It was a feeling, a message coming to me with the voice of the drum, coming down the staff, speaking in the whirr of the feathers, breathing in the smoke of the fire, the smell of the burning cedar. I felt the drumbeat in my heart. My heart became the drum, both beating and beating and beating. I heard things. I did not know whether to believe what the voice told me, what Grandfather Peyote told me. Even now I cannot believe it. . . . The Ghost Dancers went around and around in a circle, chanting until they fell down in a swoon, leaving their own bodies, leaving the earth, wandering along the Milky Way and among the stars.

> Mary Crow Dog
> *Lakota Woman* (1990)

I will tell you one more thing, and it will be the last thing I have to say about the pipe. When this lady (Calf Pipe Woman) came and gave the Sioux the pipe, she told them to go and kill four warrior members of another tribe. They were to remove a little hair from each man's head and to tie it to the pipe. Also an ear was to be removed from one victim and attached to the pipe. Then they were to get two tail feathers from a golden eagle and tie these to the stem. They followed her orders completely, and these things are there. When I saw the pipe, the hair, brittle from age, was breaking in places, and the two feathers were so worn away that only the quills remained. The ear was still in perfect condition, although it was as white as tanned deer skin.

> Frank Fools Crow in
> Thomas E. Mails
> *Fools Crow* (1979)

CRAZY HORSE IN STILLNESS

CONTENTS

Scaffolds:

DAKOTA MEMORY

The Migration

my nose buried in its fur I sleep
its fur wet it smells of dung & grass
it moves with its herd this night stars scroll
in horns its herd moves, but slowly, but moves
my animal eats stars in the wet grass
I cling to its wet fur I sleep athrill
in the smells of my animal

Before

The snow has melted. Under a warm spring sun
buffalo crop grass without looking up,
their small eyes half-hidden in hair.

Prairie is again remembering flowers.
Bees in flowers. Colors in flowers.
The herd eats its way slowly across prairie,

no one here to see them. This is before,
this is before the human hunters,
tens of thousands of years before, when,

sun now directly overhead, clouds gather
& rain rains again on prairie,
as it has for days before, & will the next,

as buffalo graze in rain, tasting
the wet grass, rain running from fur
in rivulets as they crop the new grass,

as flowers bead with rain,
& bees bumble among petals that tremble
in prairie showers. No one will see them here

for tens of thousands of years,
flowers budding & blooming in rain
as prairie continues its reawakening.

Snow Maggots

This herd frozen dead in its canyon,
every animal. Soon,
the hatchlings. . . .

No one, snow now melting from carcasses,
passes here to hear this
maggoty hum,

or, as hides burst open in spring heat,
to see them in their glistening.
The maggots feast,

some—those that survived the bone herd
to reach us in our own day—
borne off

in the bellies, feathers, & fur
of scavengers.

The Calves

A buffalo cow licks its new calf,
flies abuzz around them this late afternoon
of windless sun. The calf steadies itself
from the gentle force of its mother's tongue.

Exhausted, but she licks her calf until
her tongue & the warm sun dry its coat,
& the new animal, one of hundreds of thousands
swelling the herds these days, bawls & nudges

up under her. This is before,
this is occurring a thousand years before
homo sapiens appears on the prairie horizon. For now,
sun crosses sky, flowerheads follow,

bees find the flowers, thousands of calves
suck their mothers for that milk so thick
with prairie cream. Rumps twitch, tails swish
flies from legs & hindquarters, the herd

eats its way across the land, maybe a white moon
in the day sky watches, but that's all, maybe
wolves' eyes & a white moon, but that's all,
no human presence here as calves are born

or are they licked into shape by their mothers,
the few sickly calves that will feed the wolves,
the tens of thousands of healthy calves that will herd.
This was, this went on for longer than we can possibly

imagine, before the first human being
first heard the herd from a distance,
then set foot here. Will it never
not be before? So many animals herd here

that the moon itself may feel it inconceivable
that anything will ever change. The calves' fur
now riffles in slight wind just beginning,
clouds are forming, in the distance thunder

beats its arhythmic drum, rain
will soon soak the grasses & flowers, rain
will puddle in hoofprints for a hundred centuries,
& a hundred more, & more. Nothing is eternal

if not these calves that seem always, ever
since moon broke away, since ocean
receded like dust into the future,
to have been born here, before.

The Birth of Crazy Horse

On the morning after three days' fast,
Crazy Horse reached a gemstone the size of a lodge,
& walked in. Inside, a path wound
to a tree veined into stone, its branches scaffolds,
its heart a shape-shifting nest from which—

now he inclines his head—music smokes. No reason
not to rest, & wait for his people
to find this gemstone lodge. *Wakan Tanka*
creates itself in this tree, while
he listens for himself soon to be sung. . . .

These Seeds

Buffalo graze in low grass in this valley of scattered sunflowers
whose heads bend high as the calves' chests.
The sunflowers hear the herd & rumblings of thunder. Wind

increases, ruffling fur, swaying blooms on their stems, carrying
smells of the herd. One animal comes to a yellow head,
eats the stem, the head falls, seeds fall out, hooves

press seeds into moist ground, & now rain veils this valley
of grazing beasts where, in ten thousand years, human
blood will seep into roots of flowers descended from these seeds.

Objet d'Art

Mid-April 1873 Elizabeth Custer stepped down
from her Pullman onto Dakota plains.
Before tents were pitched, she & other wives attached
to the 7th Cavalry gathered household belongings &,

"in a little stockade made of chests and trunks,"
enclosed a family of puppies, several older dogs,
& canaries & mocking birds in their cages.
"We set out, making ourselves a temporary home,"

but soon a blizzard hit, she couldn't see
her white hands in front of her, much less
the gigantic herd of buffalo edging
this night's sleep: the animals stand wedged—

calves & cows behind, bulls toward tumultuous snow—
until the whole herd appears in a glacier,
a moment of crystal:
thousands of beasts suspended in a paperweight. . . .

Elizabeth Paints Iron Horse

Wore on his shoulders a cape trimmed with ermine.
Leggings and moccasins a mass of bead-work.
All Indian hair, as his, is straight and black.

Cap of otter without a crown. Hair wound
with strips of fur hanging down his back.
All Indian hair, as his, is straight and black.

Three eagle feathers fastened to his scalp-lock
to stand erect. Armlets of burnished brass.
All Indian hair, as his, is straight and black.

From each ear, many earrings depending.
Buckskin neckline fringed with scalps,
several of which are light and wavy.

Sepulchral Boughs

We passed an ancestral tree,
a burial place for the Indians.
I counted seventeen
lashed to boards and laid across

the main branches, and there
so securely fastened
that even a violent storm
could not dislodge them.

Elizabeth Meets Star-of-the-North

Elizabeth once bowed to an Indian so deeply
her head touched the pommel of her saddle:
"I meant, if politeness would propitiate,
not to be deficient in that quality
at such a critical moment."

The Quiver

Later, Custer & his officers remembered him—
Cheyenne, a powerful & forbidding warrior
armed with a thick bow, already strung,
& quiver of iron-pointed arrows.

All during the tense scene when one
inadvertent move would have caused
much bloodshed, he stood unexcited,
but not unmindful of surrounding danger.

Holding his bow in one hand, with the other
he continued to draw from his quiver
one arrow after another, examining each,
first casting his eye along the shaft to see

if it was true; then, with finger & thumb,
gently feeling along the point & edge
of the barbed head, returning to the quiver
any that could not be trusted. As you will, here.

Wedding Reception

Libbie's winter dream soldiers at the post
spend days digging a square pit to contain

countless carcasses & skid river ice
for its bottom & cut iceblocks

for its walls to the surface of the ground layers
of dead warriors covered with straw covered

with icepicked ice through which gaudy
feathers poke like flowers at last a pyramid

erected over this locker to freeze this meat
until at least her golden anniversary.

Custer, Around a Civil War Campfire

1. (Cannibals)

Custer, around a campfire, heard of the flesh-eaters,
the Tonkaways—how they cut from a captive
parts of his calves & thighs, place these on coals

to broil. When an artery or large vein is severed,
the flow of blood is stanched by searing with a brand,
until the most delicious flesh has been consumed.

2. (Corpse Evidence)

If a body is pierced with many bullet holes or arrows,
or cut & slashed with deep careless gashes,
the spirit passed before the Indian got possession,

but artistic dissections, partial flayings, dislocations,
breaking & splitting of bones, indicate that the victims
died with all the pain that their devils could devise.

Echoes

Though this was far from etiquettical,
once, in New Orleans, in a restaurant,
encouraged by the General,
a chef startled Libbie with a turtle,
flipped it onto their table. The long-necked,

green, scrubbed, ill-tempered reptile
bore its own epitaph on its undershell:
I shall be served for dinner on Sunday.
The turtle was about as old as they,
the chef explained, indicating tell-tale swirls

in plastron that echoed eyes in a dream
of Indians Libbie had had the night before.
Custer chortled, but his "iddle dirl"
could not recover her peaches & cream
demeanor for the duration of their meal.

Slush

Hail fell from a clear blue sky
straight down in the windless day.
Custer flicked slush from his hatbrim,
damned if this wasn't the damnedest place.

Who could believe millions of flowers
lifting from slush sleep into such
a hot sun? Out here, everything happened
at once, the gospel, God's word verbatim.

Old Testament

The best robes came from young cows
killed in late autumn when
winter coats were short & thick.

From posts on the Missouri
the American Fur Company
sent furs downriver. The Indians

drank blood & ate livers raw while
Easterners huddled under robes,
reading the West from their bibles.

LDS

Mormon caravans found green seeps of oil
along the Oregon Trail,
& greased their wagon wheels.

Sage was sharp & pungent as hot asphalt
as the emigrants cut
into that desert predicted on gold tablets.

White & Gold

Curly & his friend Lone Bear found a white man dead.
In a sack hung around the neck, two stones
of the yellow stuff. He'd seen hundreds of these people
headed over the mountains. Some came back, some
got trapped in snow & ate one another, these whites.

White Powder

Gotten from the trader. To be left
outside the horse herd
on pieces of meat in colting time
to poison wolves. It seemed right,
to protect mares & their young,

to offer this choice to the ravenous.
But when wolves died & diminished to bones,
where, then, Crazy Horse wondered,
was the white powder? For every star
that streaked in one direction in the heavens,

another streaked another, & was answered
by another. Who conceived
this cursed powder? The whites.
Lakota breathe it, eat it, die from it,
who should be watching the herd.

Peace Papers

Little Eagle, Cheyenne elder whose son
married that moon into the Oglalas,
hunted a gully for deer, out alone,
his ears not what they'd been—
two soldiers in moccasins were upon him. . . .

This was during the time of the peace papers
when Crazy Horse was the boy Curly.
At Laramie, soldiers showed white emigrants
Little Eagle's scalp, his blue medicine stone
still tied into hair: gasps of fearful pleasure.

Intimations

Crazy Horse knew a warrior who, day & night,
dug a hole. Children watched, the hole deepened
& slanted off, the warrior dug out a cave for himself,
there where the sun could not angle in. . . .

From their other world, the dead found him. Crazy Horse
heard communion upwelling in murmurs, himself
sometimes their subject. He knew he needed to shape
a cave in his own chest, to learn to welcome

the ones fighting toward him through roots & rocks
for when he'd be travelling with them.

Before the ink was dry.

Sympathetic Magic

On the day called December 31, 1866, when his friend Lone Bear
died in his arms, breast a lump of blood from a bluecoat bullet,
Crazy Horse contracted to hate. To patient hate. His heartbeat
speeded, slowed, & then slowed to slower than Lone Bear's.

The Slowing

White Bull, Rain-in-the-Face, Flat Hip & Brave Bear
all thought they might have killed Custer.
Red Horse said an unidentified Santee killed Custer.
Yes, all these, but maybe Sitting Bull's dream

of soldiers falling headfirst into his campfires
killed Custer. Yes, but maybe Crazy Horse's trance
slowed Custer down, slowed him down at last
to slower than slow motion for the kill.

Dam

Crazy Horse saw the big-teeth build a dam.
Day after day they worked until done.
I, too, would build such a dam,
he thought. I would not build it of trees,

but of the bones of the whites, rib & limb-bones,
& skulls, countless skulls to stare out
into the water. Let fish nest in those cavities
& turtles clean off any clinging meat.

The Sioux Watch the First White Man Demonstrate His Weapon

It was made of iron,
& was heavy,
& not a bow,
but a hollow rod.

He shook black sand
into the iron, then
placed an iron ball
on the end.

He forced the ball
down with a stick
pulled out from under
the hollow iron.

He pressed this stick
onto the ball, then
pushed the ball
to the lower end.

He withdrew the stick
& put it back
where it was, then
shook more

of the black sand
into a little cup
on the side of the iron, then
covered up the sand

with a flat, crooked piece
attached to the iron.
Behind this crooked piece
was a flat piece of stone

made to strike fire
when he pulled on a wire
under the hollow iron.
When this stone made fire,

that noise was heard,
& fire & smoke
exploded from the end
of the hollow iron.

None could see
the iron ball
as it flew to its mark,
& some who watched

said that the ball
struck the tree
before the fire
shot from the iron.

Wagon Gun

The boy heard a warrior say he'd seen
one of the soldiers' guns fire just one shot
into antelope passing the fort:

just one shot ripped up many animals
so that only crows could eat their pieces,
others' faces were partly blown away,

many were blinded or with broken legs tried
to crawl off through a mist of fur & blood
over a space of earth three lodges around.

Snuff

When the Sioux first heard a musical snuffbox,
its tinklings of strange formal melody,
they thought that a tiny white man
must be hidden inside,
& he was.

Crazy Horse Mnemonic

When the heavens thunder, it is the herds, or thunder.
When the herds thunder, it is the heavens, or the herds—
dark brown & black over the sacred land, the color of sound.

When the ground thunders, it is the herds of the heavens.
When the heavens thunder, it is the herds of the ground—
dark brown & black over the sacred land, the color of sound.

The herds thunder across the heavens. The herds
thunder over the ground—dark brown & black, black
& dark brown over the sacred land, the color of sound.

The Cord

When Curly was seven, his parents gave him
a turtle amulet containing,
packed in seeds,

his birth-cord. He could open the turtle,
push his fingers through seeds
& hold the small hoop.

He'd stare at it a while, until the turtle would tell him
to return the cord to its belly & clasp
its shell closed.

X Ray

When Curly was ten, he had his feet
measured for shoes with a machine.
Against a bluegreen background,
his bones glowed. With his brain,

he wiggled his toes: down there, ghostly
toe-bones wiggled. The salesman
pointed his pointer & closed the deal
with Curly's father. The half-

life of trauma is forever, except
that ignorance helps but
Crazy Horse isn't. Each step
of his mind radiates forward

as cancer bides its time,
or doesn't. But how deadly it was,
& beautiful, just once, to see his bones
move like spirits with his mind.

Pollen

Curly wove a cage from willow twigs,
dropped it over a bumblebee.
Bee bumbled & buzzed,
lifted itself as best it could
to the closed sky of its lodge,
tried to force the sides,
but could not get out. . . .

All day Curly stroked it with flowerstems,
spoke to it, asked for its medicine,
for bee was fat with the waxy
yellow droplets of the moon of new grass.
It seemed to hear him, & promise.
When he lifted away the cage, bee
flew twice around him & away.

The boy found a tiny bit
of that yellow stuff, left behind.
It dissolved on the tip of his tongue
against the back of his top teeth.
For an instant, he saw what the heavy-
laden bee saw as it flew
over the land of the Lakota.

Desire

Sometimes, in the dust & slow surge of humps,
the white speck was visible, & sometimes not.
This time, when the herd browsed close enough
to Curly & his friends quiet at the edge

of the timber, they all saw it, clearly,
the white calf, & wanted to follow it, & wanted
to capture it, & wanted to slay & taste it, & wanted
to leave it be. When one boy cried out,

the herd stampeded. That night, a theme
spread through the camp. The old ones nodded—
they had lived that visionary childhood—
& Boy Who Cries Out received his name.

Body Language

Before running, Curly pressed his palm against his chest,
then ran to the talking trees beside the river, then
stopped & felt for his heartbeat again.

Slow, fast, before & after—something inside him was wiser than he was,
& he was glad. Nor would he ever not be amazed:
here in the trees the leaves

received their motions from something invisible, & spoke that language
closest to his while he was dreaming. Now, even
while running back, he'd sleep,

& feel what rhythm his heart would shape of him,
entire, & feel what rhythm his heart
would shape of him.

His Song

On September 3, 1855, the year of Whitman's transcendental bible
Leaves of Grass, after attacking a Brule village north of the Platte,
General Harvey's soldiers bayonetted pubic hair

from dead squaws. The boy Curly saw the mutilated women. "These tend
inward to me, and I tend outward to them," wrote the poet.
Curly wove his song from everything he knew.

Bowl

Curly's mother's mother
had been known for her pottery.
Now, were there among the people any
who could make such a bowl of earth & sky
as he held in his hands? One night,
he walked around inside it under trees
beside a river. Underfoot,

a turtle made of the trader's metal
flared into sharp edges, then
cut him, or bit him. Even mud
could not stop the bleeding until
he bled a rivulet that diffused
into the rust of dawn,
his grandmother's bowl broken.

Thespians

At peace pow-wows
Indians wore clothes stripped
from slain bluecoats,

&, often, their scalps.
Still, the whites pretended
to listen & converse.

Musket Dragon Sleep

Flintlock with a three-foot barrel,
sturdy, light, deadly at close range,
Curly's first gun.

Large trigger-guard, brass lockplate
on which a dragon rears up in sea-waves
over rocks on a shore.

The boy fingers & tongues this scene
hundreds of times until
he wakes the monster that breathes fire,

the villages burned & devoured
by that alien creation of the whites.
The moon, too, or was it the sun,

or was it another planet, shone
from out there where world fell off
into the mouth of sleep.

Being

Curly finds himself
gazing up at himself
from the depth of a pond.
I am this, then,
he repeats to himself.
The boy in the pond
mimics his every face,
but how can he mind?
Is this confusion,
or is it clear
that water is air,
air is water?
His watery twin,
here, there,
looks up in wonder
into this other.

The Body

When Curly wrestled, which arms & legs were his?
As he kept wrestling himself, he couldn't lose.
How many families in the village's many lodges?
To understand this was to understand everything.

Meditation

Curly veered to a dark spot in the snow,
dug into it. The dead owl clutched
two pinecones in its claws. This puzzle

puzzled the boy. This hunter of mice & rabbits,
this leaver of bone & hair pellets,
carrying seedcones? Where going,

what doing the instant it died? He'd save
one seed, & plant it. He'd climb
that tree into light, & return with answers.

Power

A bobcat leapt
over Curly's wickiup,
its shadow did not.

The boy slept
inside that shadow until,
even by sunrise

the bobcat had not
returned for it,
Curly's to keep.

Hunger Cadet Hangover Animals

Custer, hoping to down a square meal in the mess-hall
the morning after various debaucheries,
wondered how the hell

he'd get that term paper in on time.
The red race about whom
he was writing

seemed to swirl in his stomach, their plains
a multicolored primitive mix
of horsemanship

& regal eagle plumes & bear grease smeared
in the red bucks' stinking hair.
The buffalo

& sickly-erotic visions of doe-soft women wallowed in him.
He needed a latrine, on the double,
to come clean

on questions of savage impediments to civilization.
He'd get out there some day
to have his way

& eat some god-damned decent chow beyond this West Point
chipped prairie dog shit
on toast.

Collective Unconscious

Little George in Sunday school when asked
what part of the Bible he liked best said
"the fightenest part," & as to whom
he'd most like to meet in heaven,

"Goliath." The Jungian kid
sped home with stories in his head
within which Crazy Horse, rapid eyes moving
slingshot vice-versa, deconstructed.

Feathers

Curly sat in a pit covered with branches.
He'd tied a skinned rabbit near where
he could reach his arm through to seize
the eagle he hoped would visit him here.
He kept watch. He wrestled his ten fingers.
Some kind of time went by within which
he wondered how he'd protect his eyes. . . .

In later years, he'd often finger the chest scar
its beak had gouged, & feel its wings
sweep his eyes closed. . . . His own wrist seemed
talons & feathers aswirl in outraged voice.
When it was over, he lay bloodied & exhausted
among the rocks, his own wings spread,
his head still hearing the eagle's cries.

Owl Winter

That worst winter,
as crystalline snow deepened against his father's lodge,
Curly raised the nestling owl he'd found
while gathering kindling,

fed it pemmican
& a watery mash of berries. The snow deepened,
the owl grew, friends laughed & wondered
to watch it flare

& hiss from its perch
when anyone but the boy approached.
One stupid affectionate puppy
wanted to play with it

& got a faceful of claws,
but at night the owl's aura shimmered, its eyes
reflected in least light & knew
where Curly was. . . .

So it went on,
snow deepened against Crazy Horse's lodge long before
Curly received that name, & the owl
might have been a dream,

but wasn't: every frozen morning,
the boy woke to find it in its place. Nor will there ever not be
an ending to this, he thought, as the owl,
all those lengthening days,

tested its wings.

Patriot 1890

************Two miles from Wounded Knee,
************a boy heard rifle & cannon shots.
************Arrived at the slaughter, he found
among the other bodies a dead baby
whose bonnet bore a beaded American flag.

Dakota Memory

His father showed him where
sunflowers returned each year

from villagers of centuries before,
& Curly could not stay away from here:

flowerheads hunched down from bent necks
as though to tell where those others were,

& whorls of yellow ears could hear him,
he was certain, & were certain he'd return.

They nodded, not one but the whole field,
these nomads rooted in the land of home

where Crazy Horse is buried each year
amid the myriad sunflowers.

Heartwood:

EVENING HEART ANGEL ASCENSION

The Thought

The thought kept growing in him.
It was already short grass, & would be eye-high
before another sleep. The thought climbed,
took on color, a pink flower color,
unbudding, circling a stem of tall grass,

& Crazy Horse liked the way the thought grew,
whatever thought it was. Whatever thought it was
was less important, less certain than the feel
of motion in his head: this thought
growing & filling with the color of a pink flower.

The Key

Plebe Custer perused his grammar text.
Independent clauses held his interest.
Such units acted on their own,
eschewing attachment or conjunction.
Declarative statement is the key,

decisiveness the sentence's basic structure:
noun, verb, object—direct or indirect—
strict Roman phalanx, or cavalry charge
whose power fulfills the first rule of usage:
kick ass—the subject being yourself, & understood.

Fast

Crazy Horse saw an arrow in the light
above his lodge, thin shaft of darkness
with head of green stone, seeming to streak
toward whatever target, but staying.

When he rubbed his eyes & opened them again,
the arrow remained. When he harkened
to the other five directions, then back again
to this speeding stillness in the air,

the arrow turned its head to him, pointed
at his breast, then, in a burst of glare, disappeared.
If he was not himself the intended one . . .
If he was not himself that head of green stone . . .

The Return

As he surfaced from his trance,
objects became distinguishable around him,
losing, at the same time, their namelessness.
But trees withdrew what they'd been saying,
rocks regressed to their eyelessness,

& Crazy Horse inhabited himself again,
wondering where he'd been,
& for how long. His chest ached with meaning,
but what was it? He knew
everything the world needed to know:

this. He stood up
& began walking, first one step & then another.
The people of his village
could feel him coming toward them,
one step at a time.

Earring

Crazy Horse wore one intricate silver earring,
something like a gyroscope, & filled
with tiny filigrees of aerial.

When he slept on his heart side, it covered his ear.
His dreams sometimes heard ahead
even as far as the last shot

he himself would fire into our future, but further:
the earring hummed as the sleeper
traveled to out here

where time is a matter only of rest, of almost
inconceivable rest....
Leaf fall

or solar flare, Crazy Horse, you always knew,
didn't you?—how everything exists
because at least

one sleeper listens to time
in a silver
earring.

Rot

Flesh side up, skins were stretched, scraped, shaved thin,
rubbed with a mixture of tallow & brains,
left for sun & wind to dry, then

the best robe painted & given back to the hunting grounds. Over time,
earth accepted the robe: maggots & insects,
then mice & small birds,

then raptors that took these, & then the sky. In the end, the last
patches of fur vanished downward into that place
where the herds were conceived.

The Keeping

Before the Battle of the Wilderness, May, 1864,
her beloved wrote to reassure his Libbie,
"On the eve of every battle in which I have been engaged,
I have never failed to commend myself to Destiny's keeping.

"After having done so, all anxiety for myself is dispelled.
I feel my destiny in the hands of a Higher Power.
This belief, more than any other fact or reason,
makes me brave and fearless as I am."

Custer to His Sister, April 20, 1862

Day before yesterday we buried our dead
in the clothes they wore when killed,
each wrapped in his blanket. No coffins.
It seemed hard, it could not be helped.

One, shot through the heart, had been married
the day before he left Vermont. Just as his comrades
were about to consign his body to the earth,
I thought of his wife, and not wishing to put my hands

in his pockets, cut them open,
and found his knife, wallet and ring.
I then cut off a lock of hair
and gave these to a friend of his from the same town

who promised to send them home.
As he lay there, I thought of that poem—
"Let me kiss him for his mother"—and wished
his mother were there to smooth his hair.

Remembrancers

(May 14, 1864)

After carnage & victory, he sent his Elizabeth
sprigs of honeysuckle plucked at Richmond.

(Letter to Elizabeth, 1873)

I have a fine buffalo head for you, beautifully
haired and with symmetrical horns.

The Animal

Sometimes, to breathe his own inhuman breath, Crazy Horse
wrapped his face in fur, breathed full chests of air
until the other world appeared. . . .

In breath-fur or -feather, he knew he'd been here before.
More than once, he'd been an animal, but
which?—*buffalo* or *bear,*

*eagle elk wolf coyote duck raccoon porcupine antelope hawk
rabbit wolverine wildcat snake?* . . . His own breath,
yes, but an other's, or others':

a being or beings that flew, or swam, or lived under rocks. . . .
He'd fall asleep, wake to deep lungfuls
of cooler air, the fur loose

about his face, whatever animal it was escaped
until the next time its human host
breathed it into being.

The Mystical

A rift in the clouds, the moon, & Crazy Horse sees,
in the leaves of a cottonwood, a being,
himself. How did he grow there,

& did he see himself here, & was he there, now,
asking himself the same questions
about that other self

beneath the tree? Was this his dream, or was the tree
dreaming him there, or here?
Whichever,

the moon seemed to name everything holy, & the tree
answered with silver leaves
& his own face. . . .

He did not have to know, he knew. Clouds & the moon
& the living tree humming in his head
& moon humming the tree . . .

Toilette

As Custer wiped his butt with a reb corncob,
a minie whistled over,
cutting a leaf or three. Nothing personal,
he chanced, & continued. . . .

Shaved with Libbie's gilt-framed gift of a mirror.
Wind billowed the tent
from which it depended from golden cords. His face
sliced into slivers of sunlight. . . .

Spat out baking soda brushings onto an ant-mound.
The curious pismires
sipped the stuff, & tasted him, & liked it, & why
wouldn't they again? . . .

Washed his cock with campfired water the warmth of which
pleasured him. He splashed
another cupful & lathered to why he'd like to die
like this, cum-Libbie. . . .

Puritan Angels

1. (George to Elizabeth, August 1864, from Virginia)

The day before yesterday, we had a severe engagement. . . .
During the whole time I never used a single oath.
My staff spoke of it afterwards. This is the first time
I have not been remarkably profane during the heat of battle.

2. (Elizabeth to George, August 1864, from Washington)

The best news was of your having successfully
overcome the fearful habit of using oaths.
I feel that the angels in heaven
sang glad songs over your victory.

Faith

George wondered if souls knew much more now
than when alive. Odds were their new estate
baffled them—chasms of bodiless images—

unless the dead bivouacked on another planet
with twice the gravity of earth's. Before the war,
he knew a story that explained everything, and still

sometimes almost believed, as though an oriole
sang in his breast—as one did in Elizabeth's.
He'd marry her and keep that celestial door ajar.

Scherzo Honeymoon Incident, 1864

"The gloomiest, most care-worn man I ever saw,"
the President shook Elizabeth's hand, let go,
then heard her name & took her hand again: "So,
this is the young woman whose husband goes

into a charge with a whoop and a shout. Well,
I suspect he won't be doing so any more."
Libbie replied that she hoped he would! "Oh,"
Abe laughed, "then you want to be a widow."

The Fashion

Those were ignominious days for women—
thank fortune they are over when,
for custom, we disfigured ourselves
with the awkward waterfall,

and, no matter how luxuriant one's hair,
one seemed required to still pile up more.
With many wrathful opinions regarding the fashion,
my husband one day took the hairpins, net and switch,

and thrust them into the breast of his coat.
When another officer spied out my accoutrements,
the General scoffingly referred to them
as "dead women's hair."

The Gelding

A Cheyenne medicine man told Crazy Horse,
"The things the soldiers do to our women
geld a man," & Crazy Horse himself had found

in the possession of dead soldiers the dried
scalped inner lips of Indian women. . . .
He had loved Black Buffalo Woman since childhood,

even after she'd married, but now, thinking of her,
could not rise to full moon in his chest
without those lips bleeding behind his eyes.

National Debt: Custer to Elizabeth from Virginia, 1864

When I think of the sacrifices you have made for me,
the troubles and trials you have endured to make me happy,
the debt of gratitude you have placed me under,
my heart almost fails me to think I have only
the devotion of my life to offer you in return. . . .
While I was in the thickest, with bullets whistling by me
and shells bursting all around me, I thought only of you.

The American Civil War

The blood & piss
& the lock of hair sent home
with a white rose, & gangrenous

suppurations, breeches filled with the dead's shit,
& the lock of Ramseur's hair Custer sent home
to his enemy's beloved wife who had just birthed

their first child,
a daughter,
a lock of hair & a white rose,

& Custer at Appomattox as Colonel Newhall sketched him,
"Custer of the golden locks, his broad sombrero
turned up from his bronzed face, crimson cravat floating

over his shoulders, gold galore
spangling his jacket sleeves,
a pistol in his boot,

gangling spurs on his heels, a ponderous Claymore
swinging at his side—a wild daredevil of a General,"
in front of thousands of blue-clad troops,

ordering his band to play
"Battle Hymn of the Republic,"
& then he sees General Robert E. Lee

stepping down the McLean House steps, majestic—
in one historian's words, "radiating a solemn grandeur
with his trim silver-white beard and noble stature,

immaculately garbed
in an untrimmed gray
full-dress uniform buttoned

to the throat, his ornaments a beautifully embroidered
red-and-yellow sash, gold spurs, gold-sheathed sword,
his hands encased in glowing white gauntlets"—

&, since this is
the American Civil War
preserved in annals of roses

& dysentery & punctured lungs & brain-splattered
blinded faces & written in perfume on lavender-
scented *billets-doux* carried over the moonlit killing fields,

Custer, as General Grant
tips his shabby fedora
to salute Lee, & the rebel

raises his gray immaculate brim respectfully,
murmurs to his bandmaster that word, you know the word
above all, not *death*, not *love*, not *flag*, not *futility*,

not *honor*, not *stupidity*, not *slavery*,
not *delusion*, not *beauty*, not *union*
or *secession*, but one word

comprised of these & more, & the bandmaster signals,
that word's sound fills peaceful Virginia countryside,
I wish I was in Dixie: / Hoorah! hoorah! / In Dixieland

I'll take my stand,
To live and die
in Dixie . . .

& in these woods ravens glut themselves on viscera,
beetles roll balls of dung through caged hearts twined
with music & roses in the shattered starlight ecstasy

of *Dixie* where we take our stand,
to live & die
in *Dixie. . . .*

Custer Declines to Sit for a Marble Bust

Custer writes the famous sculptress, "Your victories
are lasting and, unlike mine, not purchased
at the cost of life-blood of fellow creatures—leaving
sorrow, suffering, and desolation in their track."

Pralines

Custer's spiffed up in tux & spats but
out-of-place among civvie luminaries,
handkerchief soaked with his vet's sweat.
The dessert drones on, war consecrated

in flowery bombast while the dead
sour the ground from Bull Run to Shiloh,
& beyond. Once, twice, he cuts his eyes
into Libbie's. They stand, & get the hell out.

The Decision

Libbie in a meadow a child is hanging
in air suspended from nothing in green sunlight
in swaddling. Others run to this child but

Libbie pleads, "Don't, don't touch it,
it might fall"—she thinks invisible threads
might be holding it. After a long heartbeat,

she's near enough to cradle it in her palms,
& lift it until it cleaves to her breast,
so warm, & safe now, & hers to give away.

Disequilibrium

When only a thousand buffalo were left alive on the plains,
one old bull hid inside a tree, crossed its growth rings
inward toward dead heartwood where it somehow knew
it would have to live. Each year the tree added a ring,

& each year the buffalo receded further toward its future.
Meanwhile, from beyond the riverbank where the tree lived,
soldiers were galloping toward him with politicians
& lawyers & dozers & cement trucks on their shoulders.

Signals

                    Moist gunpowder smeared on a wet arrowhead,
             & lighted, & by how high or low it arced,

& its direction across the night sky,

             & by duration between arrows, & now in the context
                    of railroad, telegraph, & cavalry.

George Belden: The Simplest Form

Some wild Indians
wear a steel
or iron ring
in the scalp-lock,
the hair being plaited
around the ring
in such a way
that it cannot
be removed, unless
the hair is unbraided

or the scalp-lock
cut off. I have
often removed the ring
by taking off
a piece of the scalp,
which is the simplest form
of getting it.

The Wallow

Circumstances were these:
Sergeant Bain, while out
following Indians after the battle,
on the third of September, 1863,
came upon a buffalo wallow
filled with sick & wounded enemy,
some in a dying condition.
With a ferocity unparalleled,
he sprang into the wallow,
tomahawked twenty-seven of the Indians
with their own weapons,
& scalped them with their own knives.
He did this, he said, in revenge
for the squaws cutting the tongues out
of our wounded the night before.

Subsequent Events

So as not
to allow the savages to locate
and disinter our slain comrade
and take his scalp,
we buried him at night
under tethered horses
so that their tramping
should obliterate all traces
of his final resting place.
No use.

After the Fetterman Massacre, 1866: Woodcutters

A dozen wagons returning to the fort
with cottonwood & willow limbs not
hard or dry enough for much except
to dispel the chill. Deadwood best,
when handy & not yet gone to rot. . . .

The wagons deepen ruts in woods just
on the verge of thaw. A dust of snow,
sifting. The fort in sight, your heart
slows in its chest. Relief. For now,
at least, Indian eyes retreat.

The Gun: A Romance

A year after Fetterman, skeletons of horses & mules,
human bones, pieces of skulls, knapsacks, torn uniforms,

& broken guns lay scattered over the area
for a mile or more. George Belden picked up

a flintlock Indian gun bearing the rusted designation
"London, 1777." For a moment, he closed his eyes:

How many battles had it seen, where had it traveled,
how many wild animals, Indians, and white men slain?

The Count

Crazy Horse counted cottonwood leaves along the river,
realizing one leaf for each buffalo,
& those just appearing in the spring of this dream

were calves being born. If he could keep the trees
from the whites, the herds would thunder,
so he watched the buffalo trees until their colors

wavered dark & light in the running wind....
If he could keep his rootedness, there,
he could shade his people, here.

Allies

Crazy Horse sees a child placed on the ground
by two lightning hands reaching from a cloud.
The child seems human, but is green,
the deep green of grass in the first warm moons.
Bears & wolves surround this child for protection,
& the warrior sharpens his knife on a stone.

Unknown

Custer desired the Indians "be completely humbled."
We suppose, in the end, some were & some were not.
Some of the living were humbled, & some were not.
Some of the dead were humbled, & some were not.

In 1868, Major Elliott & his men were wiped out.
General Custer asked Dr. Lippincott to report
on the character & number of wounds received by each,
as well as to mutilations to which they had been subjected.

"Sergeant-Major Walter Kennedy, bullet hole in right temple,
head partly cut off, seventeen bullet holes in back and two in legs."
By the time of his death, quick or drawn-out,
the Sergeant-Major may or may not have been completely humbled.

"Corporal Henry Mercer, bullet hole in right axilla,
one in region of heart, three in back, eight arrow wounds in back,
right ear cut off, head scalped, skull fractured, throat cut"—
the Corporal may or may not have been completely humbled.

It's a long list. It ends with those unidentifiable:
"Unknown, head cut off, body partially destroyed by wolves."
"Unknown, scalped, skull fractured, three bullet holes
and thirteen arrow holes in back." Maybe, at the exact

instant of his death, each forever-to-be-Unknown
was completely humbled, . . . but maybe not. Those of us
now scanning the report for intuitions & familiar names
must be completely humbled. Some are & some are not.

In Texas,

a moment of vertigo, Libbie's horse's hindlegs
in quicksand, excited shouts & directions
to rein left, right, quick cuts of her whip
until her mount finds firm footing again
above her vision of suffocation, that descent
of bones through eons of time, that widowhood.

Texas Gulliver Malaria

The General digs into an ant-mound,
anxious to learn its mechanisms.
Mazes of tunnels & chambers, patches
of fibrous white & yellow mold—he can
not make sense of it, & can

not find the queen, if there is one, not even among
thousands of eggs, some of which, translucent specks,
are being hauled over his boots.
The mound level, Custer continues digging,
to no avail. You get down into something,

& nothing's there, he thinks, & thinks the tribe
of pismires awesome as they rearrange their ranks.
A few weeks before, a column had ransacked
a linen twist of quinine. Now, again,
he dizzies as they seethe around him.

The Spider

It couldn't be he'd seen what he thought he had,
he said to Libbie: a spider as big as she:
it blocked his path along the river, but ascended
into a cottonwood, & disappeared. Yes, it couldn't be,
said Libbie, who turned her back to him, & shuddered.

Something About the Indians

Custer carried a petrified tree trunk in a wagon.
It reminded him of something about the Indians.
He'd often thumb the stone heartwood,
the marrow, but could not push through it

to taste its memory in his mind.
He wondered if savages had once taken shade
here under the primitive eye of God—
ochres & charred blacks, oranges & reds.

Stone River

Libbie dreamt
a petrified tree,
one huge petrified limb
nesting a petrified bird

singing a stone song,
flat & hard, nightlong,
under a moon petrified
in the petrified sky.

Grinding Stone

Custer threw the stone down from a wagon,
then rolled it into their garden.
He & Libbie sat down on it & guessed
how old it was, & what, if it could hear,
it had heard.

Meanwhile,
the abandoned village where he'd found it,
did or didn't exist when no one thought of it?
In any case, the stone would never again sing
its ancient song of hunts & plumpits.

Root Music

One square meter
of shortgrass prairie:
five miles of roots.
When a steel plow
first turned
the underlayer,
you could hear what one farmer called "a storm of wild music,"
such ringing & twanging.
Unturned,
the prairie sang
in the inner ear
of Crazy Horse,
nevertheless.

Surveyors

Indians pegged their own tipis, but these whites set sticks everywhere
as though staking a huge invisible tent to cover
all the land.

N

Crazy Horse came to a stake in the ground, one
of those countless driven in
on a straight line
from the Platte to above the Yellowstone
by the white called Bozeman.

Crazy Horse sat down
to imagine us in our dimension—
scaffolds of linguistic gridlock & confusion—
but primal brain
snarled with the almost-vision.

One stake, a new condition of air around it, & then
                another, & then lanes
    of moving coffins, & then, & then, & then

            only a sandy wind, & no one.

Grasshopper Sperm

Custer saw the whole bottom of a stream
covered for miles with grasshoppers.
He took off his boots & waded in,
just to walk on the wingless myriad,

to feel them between his toes.
A pod of whales would find their surfeit here,
he wondered, but then, at the instant of ejaculation,
became afraid of the powers of nature.

Home Body

Stiff in his saddle, Custer lifts up above the horn.
The grasslands, he thinks: too much wind,
too much space, too little rain, the aspect
of a great yawn, almost desert except
for game, flies, fringes of trees along the rivers,
the dead casting shade down from scaffolds
under which spirits linger, loth to depart
for that other world much like this one except
intensified, its colors deeper, edges sharper,
its necessities assuaged/tempered by bodiless ease. . . .
He'll get Libbie & himself the bejesus back east
once this damnable Indian business peters out.
Libbie's cleavages are valleys to Philly or D.C.
to kiss, enfolded by hills so soft to press.

Lily

Libbie hears George draining his lily in their privy. Later,
she'll warm his bulbs in her palms, he'll rise
like a calla at Easter.

Men at Play

Ground at the fort too flat for tobogganing,
the General & Tom & friends got dragged about
by a team of horses, & enjoyed slamming into fence rails
& into a certain rock that flipped them. From her window,
Elizabeth freaked out & prayed thanks she wasn't pregnant.

Elizabeth Considers the Hounds

The General loved his dozens of dogs,
the stag-hounds and fox-hounds.
The former rarely barked, but the latter
even attempted to bugle with the bugler.
Often, beside his soldierly figure,

a hound would absorb itself in imitation.
With lifted head and rolling eyes,
there issued from its broad mouth
notes so doleful they would have answered
for a misericordia.

The Sexes

The tribute a woman pays to beauty in any form, I paid to Byron,
but never cared for him, his upper lip lifted over such white fangs.
A greyhound's heart could be fit into a thimble. Byron
cared for the General as much as his cold soul could care for anyone,
but dear Ginnie: she was all love, she was almost human.

Aquifer

By and by the long wagon-train appeared.
Many of the covers had horns strapped to them,
and looked like weird bristling animals as they drew near.

My husband brought me a keg of delicious water
from a distant spring, my only look at clear water in years.
It washed the taste of mud from my mouth, for a time.

The Sleigh

A packing box for the body, edges cut
& sawed into scallops & curves, rude bobs
ironed by the company blacksmith, the torque
of an army wagon attached to the frail shell.

All woodwork was painted black,
& "really," wrote Elizabeth a decade later,
"its color and shape reminded one
of a little baby hearse."

Time

Elizabeth said that in Two Bears' village
she saw few young men—
these had joined the hostiles.

But an old one stood alone,
unconscious of everything, recited something
in loud, monotonous tones,

but no one was listening—all were watching
the approaching regiment. Still,
the man continued his recitation,

singing his people's deeds of valor
far back in history until this regiment entered
the present future of the singer's song.

Flattery

If we all huddled around
one of my husband's splendid camp-fires,
I was soon driven in by the smoke.
The officers' pretty little gallantries
about "smoke always following beauty"
did not keep my eyes from being blinded.

Hygiene

It is alleged that Tom Custer & several other
officers of the 7th took the mercury cure
for "contact" with infected squaws,
but army records disappeared
into the shredder.

Thistle Elizabeth

I think of a hundred kindly deeds shown to all us women
at the post, gentlemanly acts. I have known
of some so delicate

that I can hardly refer to them with sufficient tact,
and wish I might write with a tuft
of thistledown.

Misc. Mss.

Libbie often said she would have liked to have carried a tree with her
across the plains, & when, on those unshaded treks
she thought of someone she missed,

the loved one's face seemed shadowed in leaves. Trees' hues of green
approached infinity, &, in any wind at all, the creatures
continued writing themselves

like books of genealogy, or poetry: profligate beauty proclaimed each spring
when leaves unfurled; volumes of brown verses
revised on the ground each autumn.

Her Husband in Moonlight

How we longed to escape the dust
the unceasing winds took up
in straight whirling eddies, then wafted
in sheets of murky yellow
into our doors and windows,

making our eyes smart, parching
our throats raw. My husband
sent east for grass-seed,
which, with oats, were sown
repeatedly. He believed

that when the oats sprouted first,
these would protect the oncoming
leaves of grass. At all hours
he studied the soil to detect
a verdant tinge until,

one moonlit night we espied him
walking the parade ground,
waving his arms in speech.
Perhaps the moon was full
and Reason tottered on her throne;

perhaps, tired of being Mars,
my husband evolved to statesman
and thereby hoped to prod
his vegetable constituents
to faith and new career,

assisted by moonlight
to spell his speech.
But there was almost nothing, and then
this nothing died, despite
my Daniel Webster of the dust.

Association of Sensibility

Custer pulled his foot into a boot, but
something was there before him. In that instant,
he felt his own stupidity like a rattler's bite.

The Army

Appeared one day an army.
We beat kitchen tins
around our precious garden,

but the army was deaf,
or unafraid of sound—
it went on peacefully

eating every leaf in sight,
then soared off with our dreams
of radishes and beets.

Grouard: Baby Birds & Wild Turnips

The men were so hungry they ate anything.
They caught little birds and ate them,
feathers and all, not even waiting to kill them.

Four or five young birds in a nest:
the men ate them right down.
Finally I showed them some Indian turnips,

giving each one a top to know what they were,
and set them digging. It was not long before
they had plenty of wild turnips to cut their hunger.

Shadows

Crazy Horse, waiting in cottonwood shadows,
thought how the leaves quivered in his head
like words whose sounds were clear
as the leaves' edges, but meaningless, unless
this was itself the felt presence,

the source of himself, from himself the source,
shadows seeming to waver like wings
from the greensilver shudder of the leaves, & enough,
always, this land filled with food
& movements of water as wind moved the trees.

Hunger Song

Though Crazy Horse was out of sight, the elk lifted their ears. . . .
Downwind, they smelled him in their minds, & felt his prayer, *wapiti*,
arrowing into them: now they sensed which one would lose its self to him:
the chosen one began to feel, swelling inside itself, the Great Mystery,
the human praying its hunger to itself this time in time.

Savings Account

Dried meat pounded almost to powder between stones,
packed in a parfleche.
Melted tallow poured over the whole, which is kept warm
until saturated.
When cold, the parfleche is closed & tightly tied up.
Meat so prepared
keeps in good condition for a period of years.

Grouard: The Chickens

I managed to kill three prairie chickens.
I tried to induce my two companions to eat sparingly,
but they were so ravenously hungry I could not prevail.
I saved the chickens' necks, which I roasted, for myself,

and got the benefit of juice from the meat,
but those two ate the chickens raw,
were taken sick, and suffered only long enough
never to enjoy another meal.

Elizabeth Remembers Flood

Even in the uproar of the tempest,
there rang out on the air piercing our ears,
sounds that no one, once hearing, ever forgets—
despairing cries of drowning men.
We tried to scream to those dark forms hurrying by us,
that help might come farther down,

but the current grew more furious,
and we could distinguish, by the glare of lightning,
the men waving their arms imploringly
as they were swept down with tree-trunks,
heaps of rubbish, and masses of earth. . . .
At last, morning advanced. The stream

fell constantly, revealing a soldier, swollen
beyond all recognition, his drowned body embedded
in the bank where no one could reach it,
where we could not escape it,
could not keep our fascinated gaze from the
stiffened arm that stretched out entreatingly.

The Fish

In Libbie's dream all night the black river
meandered in front of her just out of reach
of her floating feet. Still, somehow, she saw
large fish, & then just one huge feathered one

above the water. She slipped into its painted eye
at the millisecond it reversed itself & swam . . .
whither?. . . *Slow, slow, please, no,*
she cried, but the fish bore her away.

Shoals

Libbie dreamed that a host of angels drowned
in evening sky above the prairie—
a plunging of wings & draperies, cerulean depths,
wailing resounding from the whole dome of creation.
The last angel held, for an instant, a spear,

or rifle, above the flood, then disappeared. . . .
She woke wondering the meaning, & that day
& for many days thereafter, gazed up imagining
those heavenly creatures washing up
against that ocean's unfathomable shore.

The Streams

In the last days of the month,
enemy fired grass around the post,
& for a time Libbie thought
all would be burnt up.
The slopes of the hills,
as far as the eye could reach,
were covered with lines of fire,
& tall sheets of flame
leapt up from the valley
or ran crackling through the timber.
The parade ground of the garrison
was so lighted up at night
that she could see to read,

& for a distance of miles
every tree & shrub
could be distinctly seen.
The crackling of the fire
sounded like the discharge
of thousands of small arms,
& the bursting of heated stones
resounded over the valley,
resembling the booming
of distant cannon.
She had never seen
so grand & imposing a sight.
For three days the flames raged
over a vast extent of country,
& then, having consumed
all the grass & dry trees,
went out, doing the families no harm,
owing to streams around the fort,
which completely checked the advance
of the destroying element.

Belden: The Warclub

The Indian warclub was shown me
that had been employed
in the massacre at Fort Kearney
in 1866 to break the skulls
of ninety-six soldiers and citizens.
The club is a rough stick,
the knots and end were still
clotted with blood, brains,
and human hair.

This instrument is oak,
three feet long, shaped
like a bat for playing ball,
but driven full of nails,

some bent over to form
a loop, or hook. Most of the ninety-six,
already dead, did
not know what struck them,
praise God.

Misery

In the summer of 1867, after what for Libbie
were interminable letterless weeks at Fort Riley,
arrived the clank of sabre on her gallery
& the quick spring of feet: "There before me,
blithe and buoyant, stood my husband!"

She ends *Tenting on the Plains* in reverie:
"There was in that summer one long, perfect day.
It was mine, and—blessed be memory which preserves
the joys as well as the sadness of life!—
it is still mine, for time and for eternity."

Colors: Custer Describes a War Party

The Indians were arranged in full war costume,
their heads adorned in brilliantly-colored bonnets,
some carrying the long lance with its pennant of bright colors,
their faces, arms, and bodies painted in various colors,
rendering their naturally repulsive appearance even more hideous.

Night, Sleep, Death and the Stars

When I piss I affect the world's water level,
but this kind of info ain't practical,
Custer thought, ain't something to form your credo

or take to the bank. Who babbled about what
at the Point when beer pickled tongues
at late-night bullshit sessions? Here

on the Plains the savages had been left to dream
for too long—all their myths, metaphysics, mumbo-jumbo.
Custer would be *their* nightmare, & hangover.

Before the Attack on Our Camp, 1867

Our pickets were posted as usual.
Horses and mules were securely tethered to our tents.
Guard troops had taken their stations for the night.
The bugler had sounded the signal for "Taps,"

and before the last note had died away every light,
in obedience to this command, disappeared, and nothing
remained to the eye, except here and there a faint glimpse
of a white tent to indicate the presence of our camp.

The Mouse

Custer tamed a field mouse, housed it in an inkstand
on his desk. As it ran over his head & shoulders
& burrowed his hair, it seemed fond of him,

but once, for no reason the General could discern,
that primitive creature of fur & blood
tore into his earlobe, painfully hard.

Grouse

Custer set grouse eggs under common hens, but the hatchlings
ran for cover from their domestic mothers. Kept in a coop,
they refused food, wore themselves out in futile attempts to escape,
& died. Thereafter, grouse tasted of himself to Custer.

The Antelope

On an early campaign, whenever the 7th stopped
to pitch its tents for the night, three pronghorns
made their wary way to Custer, & pawed his hand
to be petted & for grain. As they fixed on his,
theirs resembled Indian eyes. This pleased him,
& did this please him, who always seemed to himself,
& who could now deny that he was the chosen one?

Epistemology

I know something, but don't know what it is,
Custer noted to himself. He'd neared
a woodpecker hammering a canyon cottonwood,
its resonations—*blam   blamblamblam   blam*—

proving something definite to him, but what? . . .
The bird's head blurred as it wrote its monograph
in air & wood. The observer remembered,
for no reason he knew, a story he'd read

by a weird ex-cadet, a pit & pendulum
blade stroking closer to a victim's heart
each time he breathed. The bird, *blam*,
struck into cottonwood for sustenance

in this closed-in place within the limitless
plains. Custer spat, shifted his ass
in his saddle, unthought himself, dismounted,
& walked, *blam, tabula rasa* toward the tree.

Beast in Twilight

Custer a short stone's throw away,
a cow buffalo scrapes against a willow,
rasp & thrum, rubbing off old hair,
dead skin, scabs from insect bites,
in a sawing of pleasure, grunting grunts
of sublime relief, *unh, unh,* the tree
atremble, ashiver. From the mat
of the cow's fur, or the tree's bark,
or both, hovers a halo of dust backlit
by evening sun. *Unh, unh,* & birds

lift from the tree, but settle back
into its silhouette, *unh, unh,*
the birds lifting & settling, the tree
atremble, ashiver, the aura of dust
backlit by river. Custer decides
not to shoot, to do nothing except
remember the pure unselfconscious
rhythmic pleasure of the dumb beast
rubbing itself against a willow
in prairie twilight, *unh, unh.*

Evening Heart Angel Ascension

Raptor shape, or a nest, in a cottonwood.
Custer clapped. Nothing. Then put
a bullet through it. Nothing. . . .

Then, as he approached, it lifted
from the tree, huge, winged, unhurried,
silent clot of black bloodlight.

One Word

Once, when Crazy Horse knelt to a pond,
he sensed someone standing behind trees,
someone from that other life. He, alive, was
not afraid, but when he crept there,

only a shape of sound emerged, as though
a bough or birdbeak had uttered it. Still,
that one shape composed the afternoon:
the dead watched, spoke one word, departed.

Sardonics: A Brief History of the Campaign

1. (White Bread)

A box of wolf-poison hard bread thrown on a trail—
several Sioux dead from this meal.

2. (General Sherman to Libbie, 1866)

Child, you'll find the air of the Plains
is like champagne.

3. (Grasslands in the 1860s)

A settler said, "If the Indians are hungry, let them eat grass."
When soldiers found him, his mouth was stuffed with grass.

4. (Lightning, 1869)

"I will make them feel lightning," said Sheridan,
as Crazy Horse shattered lightning in a vision.

5. (Custer to Brother Tom, January 1876, from New York City)

"I expect to be in the field in the summer with the 7th,
and think there will be lively work before us."

6. (Guesswork)

When scout Bloody Knife told him
they'd find enough hostiles to fight for a month,
Custer said, "I guess we'll get through them in one day."

7. (Custer on First Seeing the Indian Encampment at Little Big Horn)

"Hoorah, boys, we've got them."

8. (A Scout's Suggestion)

"Someone better tell Yellow Hair
that the Sioux are no longer running."

9. (Apparitional)

Galloping out of the dust swirl,
horses with empty saddles.

10. (The History of Rhyme & Reason)

Though half Indian in spirit & sympathy,
Custer, instrument of Manifest Destiny.

11. (Benteen, Days Later, Standing Over Custer's Body)

"There he is, God damn him, he will never fight anymore."

12. (Victoriana)

Buffalo horns
polished into inkwells.

The Gully

That autumn, we left the territories
to spend most of the winter in New York.
We went out a great deal, once to see
a military play at Wallack's called "Ours."
When we reached the farewell scene,
and the wife's trembling hands buckled the sword
on her warrior, I could not endure it.

In February we had to say goodbye
to this pleasurable life. At Saint Paul,
the prospect was dismal, the trains would not run
before April, but they sent us through
with two snow ploughs and three enormous engines;
nevertheless, we were caught fast for days
in a gully, a desperate situation.

I wish we were there still, embedded
in ice and snow, in time, but we escaped
by sled and sped through drifts to the fort.

Forces

Crazy Horse & Custer rode through one another
emerging on the other side.
This happened in a warp of starlight
too long ago in the future to predict

or remember. For each of them,
it was as though a wind made of locusts
the size of particles of pollen, or smaller,
atoms, or smaller, had swept them

together, the exchange being . . . inevitable,
necessary, good. Crazy Horse wore
a breastplate in the shape of a butterfly,
Custer a red cravat, but these were insubstantial,

pure. The starlight wrinkles. Their horses
blink, separate, & reassemble. Then, here,
the two warriors pause to estimate their final
destinations, mount, & ride on.

Roots:

BUFFALO DUSK

Swerve

This herd extended eighty of what whites would come to call miles,
ten miles wide, grazing the shortgrass plain
under the June sun.

The great herd browsed, calves bawled, bulls drooled & kept watch,
often lifting their heads from the lush mesh.
After the births they'd given,

cows replenished themselves as the herd returned, again,
for the thousandth, the hundred-thousandth time
to the north where food

covered the rainstruck & sunstruck grounds. This day,
as always, packs of wolves slept
at the edges, the herd

swerved widely around them & kept these swerves long after
the wolves had moved to kill & sleep again
as their cubs slept & played. . . .

At night, the swerves outlined the herd under the stars,
the undulating outer line of brown beasts
now standing still in sleep

or shifting standing in this vast slow drift & flow
of animal life under those distant
points of heavenly light

that glittered from several million horns. Inside the swerves,
so much dreaming took place that earth was
otherworldly essence in which

the herd browsed, calves bawled, bulls drooled & kept watch,
often lifting their heads from the lush mesh,
cows replenished themselves,

& wolves' eyes widened & deepened into ravines into which
some of the beasts fell into teeth
waiting below. Swerve,

into sleep, swerve into awakening, everything still here,
for now, the return, the herd swerving past
where the wolves had been. . . .

Cubs

This morning the wolves had found a cripple,
had split it from the herd & killed it.
Now they lie in the grass, sated, adream,

their young ones climbing over them
on this day of warmth as prairie
awakens from its trance of snow. The cubs

play as clouds gather & rain
flicks grass about them. In their play,
they pause to see flowerheads tremble

as though in signal. The old wolves doze
through the rain until, eventually, their cubs
nuzzle beneath them for shelter, & sleep,

as the herd, the endless herd they follow,
eats its way across the spring prairie,
feeding for them on grasses & rain.

The Blessing

In the winter twilight appears . . .
Above the hidden valley appears . . .

The animals' risen breath,
& steam from their bodies,

& steam from their droppings,
& steam from their piss . . .

The frost cloud of a buffalo herd
appears in winter twilight. . . .

Blood Source

Crazy Horse saw a buffalo
on a cottonwood leaf
carried by an ant
into a hole in ground

beating like his heart
in the dreamy night lit
with enough eyes
for the herd forever.

Paunch

Two-thirds filled with water, hot stones
dropped in, removed, others dropped in
until the water bubbles, then cuts of meat

dropped in, cooked for the long remove,
the prairie itself a paunch, its stones heating,
as the village follows the herd.

Night: The Dead & the Living

In the back room of the trader's store, bales
of beaver skins are stacked against three walls,
buffalo robes against the other, floor to ceiling.
Buffalo & beaver spirits muse this stillness,
& mice punctuate with droppings.

Goes-Ahead: A Reminiscence

I was the first in battle, and the others said,
"There he goes ahead of us."

Before I was a warrior we had buffalo skulls
with the meat and skin all taken off,

and we'd tie ropes to them and put them on the ice.
The girls would sit on the buffalo heads

and we would draw them along the ice.
That was one of our greatest pleasures.

The Iron Horse

Railroad promoters proposed that a carload of buffalo bulls
be sent on an eastern tour.

Each bull was choked down, hogtied & loaded
into a railway car

with block & tackle. Of twenty-four roped & tied down,
three survived,

the others dying at various stages during the struggle, often
of broken thorax & suffocation.

During their tour of eastern cities, the three survivors
attracted much attention.

Temperance

Custer was there when the learned astronomer lectured,
the charts & graphs clarified, the heavens
laid out in grids, stars counted, moons explained,
all that vast drift & flow harnessed

into professorial conclusions & projections.
"The man's a wonder," he exclaimed to Libbie, later,
guiding her by her elbow across moist Broadway
where they ignored a drunk strung out on star-strings.

Fifth Avenue

The buffalo's ribs are wide,
spaces between them narrow, Custer knew,
so knew a phony painting when he saw one:

generic Indians arrowing an old bull's ribcage,
trailing headdresses which
they'd never have worn to hunt. The large scene,

framed in silver-filigreed plaster,
filled the whole window which drew
Manhattanites like flies to shit,

but he was too polite
to offer his critique aloud.
He leaned in like the others,

listening to their oohs & aahs, but what a bag
of bull offal
to bear such a price-tag!

Modern Art

This train was trapped in its tracks by a large herd,
front & rear & to the sides. When the animals stampeded,
the train blew its whistle, rang its bell, released its steam,
passengers fired their guns, but the herd kept on,

piling en masse against it, some jamming horns under wheels,
overturning several cars, others still piling up until
they scrambled completely over the scene,
leaving some with legs caught in broken windows.

Still Life

Last snow, & now the white prairie
flecks green & black with budding sage
visited by insects already
upspringing from thaw. A wedge

of buffalo cleaves the landscape,
moving yet staying, existing
in one place in one instant of time.
But the prairie will blossom,

non-passing instant by instant,
& the herd,
that living arrow frozen in flight,
buzzes & hums.

Catlin Painting

A buffalo bull encircled by wolves, eyes torn & bleeding,
tongue ripped off, intestines being strung out & devoured.
Still, he stands—blind, dying—& threatens his killers.

Reluctance: Grouard & the Bull Buffalo

Shooting as they got opposite me, I hit the cow,
breaking her back and killing her instantly.
The bull sniffed her dead body,
smelled the fresh blood & went crazy,

circled the cow's carcass, pawed earth,
vented terrible sounds. I lay
perfectly quiet and watched, knowing
if I made a move the bull would attack me,

and if it did, nothing would prevent my being
torn into ribbons or trampled into jelly.
For hours the infuriated bull stood over
the cow's body. I hoped to load my gun

and get one chance to kill the brute.
I managed to pour a charge of powder
from flask into palm, but the bull spied me
and rushed me. I threw myself into a washout

maybe three feet deep. I actually felt
the bull's warm breath on my neck. Unable
to reach me with its head, it raged above me
and rent the ground in its mad fury. . . .

For hours, it wore a path from the cow to me,
back and forth. I lay as dead until darkness,
when the bull departed. Many months passed
before I cared to relate this story.

Where the Herds Are Born

As Crazy Horse walked to the dead buffalo,
its eye, the one facing him, palpitated,
& kept growing. He came to that eye
higher than his head, nothing else there
to break the moonlit horizon, that eye's

pupil a door through which he walked.
Inside, riversource, a story. He tried,
later, to remember what he'd seen or done,
or what had been done to him, but couldn't,
but believed that eye in his breast from then on.

Correspondences

Custer, on horseback, first saw it from a mile distant.
"Of the hundreds of thousands of buffalo I have since seen,
none have corresponded with him in size and lofty grandeur,"
he says in *My Life on the Plains*. This was the incident

during which he shot his own horse dead: "So sudden
was this movement, so sudden the corresponding
veering of my horse to avoid attack, that to retain control
I quickly brought up my pistol hand to the assistance

of the other. Unfortunately, as I did so, my finger,
in the excitement of the occasion, pressed the trigger,
discharged the pistol, and sent the fatal ball
into the very brain of the noble animal I rode. . . ."

& now, to save wilderness & our dying world, we dwell
on that buffalo, who did circle back to the helpless general,
its brain filled with quizzical correspondences
that twinkled in its eye, before it walked away. . . .

Killing Time

At his leisure,
Custer witnessed
a curious contest
between an old bull
& several wolves
endeavoring to pull
the huge fellow down.
They tore his scrotum,
lacerated his hams,
but he still swept them
with his crippling horns.
After watching for some time,
Custer fired into the attackers—
those ran off with their hunger.
He then killed the bull, & cut
& packed its hump
for Libbie's palate.

Visit to Central Park

Custer shipped a Montana porcupine,
a cinnamon bear, & a wildcat back east
to Central Park. People would ask
where they came from, & sent by whom?

In that other life of ours, my friends,
we saw all three, if you'll only remember.
Oh, remember that sardonic look they had
when we learned of the slaughter.

Sorrow Village

Custer salvaged a medicine bundle from a burning village.
In time, he & Libbie, in the firelight of his study,
unwrapped this artifact & found, among claws & feathers
& bits of bone & beads & herbs & strips of fragrant leather,

a red stone pipe, a running buffalo carved into its bowl,
but as they held the pipe, its buffalo stopped,
looked back at them, dropped its head, then dropped
to its knees & disappeared, disappeared completely.

The Bees

A huge buffalo bull
appeared on the bluff overlooking camp,
wonderstruck at such as he'd never seen. He descended
a narrow ravine, & emerged,
& guns opened up on him. He turned & disappeared
into the ravine into which soldiers ran

to finish him off,
but the wounded animal, half crazed,
turned, met them head on, broke one's heart
with its massive head, gored two, trampled two others,
then charged into camp into a swarm
of bullets.

Dinner Bell

In '72 & '73, millions of hides,
7,000,000 pounds of tongues shipped east,

acres of carcasses blotting the grass,
afterthoughts of the Great Plains until

only bones remained, hundreds of trainloads
for fertilizer, buttons, & fine china.

Footnoted

In 1679, on a bank of the Illinois, Father Louis Hennepin
became one of the first Europeans to see
an American bison, & promptly
shot it dead.

Mushroom River

Crazy Horse picked one the size of his fist.
Underneath, gills, as in the heads of fish.
He knew it could hear him. He said,
I am going to eat you, & did,

& later, sleeping, saw himself walking
where friends he had not seen since childhood
welcomed him. To be heard, they did not need
to open their mouths. Their campfire

was a river flowing round on itself,
filled with huge silver buffalo
with red eyes. There was nothing to do here
but stare into the current, & forget, & remember.

The Hunt

In winter, you could drive buffalo into snowdrifts
half as high as the highest willows along the river,
could follow them to where they crushed one another
against the hard-packed walls of their trap. Bulls
swayed, too exhausted, by then, to move against you.

Preparing to kill, you could smell ahead to the fires,
picture people in your skull, & taste the cooking meat
even while approaching the moaning & bellowing
steam cloud. What was this hunt if not the holy
breathing in you of your own & your village's breath?

The Release

In crystalline starlight, for the first time after
the frozen moons, Crazy Horse hears water—
ice on the river at last letting loose its fingers. . . .

The same fingers, now, let loose their grip
within his head, within his breast: joy
flows in him. The herds will return.

As Best He Could

The snow kept snowing. The buffalo vanished
in their small gatherings in wood along the river.
He slept in that cold as best he could. . . .

When they opened their eyes, their eyes, just for a moment,
formed their snowy bulk into animals,
if we were there, & close enough, in starlight, to see,

but when they closed their eyes, they vanished.
Crazy Horse slept as best he could in that cold
glittery bewhited distance between himself & the life-givers.

Buffalo Sunrise

We found that place by passing through
crabapple and wild roses, we
in our leathery sweat and alkaline dust:

in a clearing, ninety skulls
painted with red and blue stripes and circles,
all facing east in parallel rows.

Buffalo Dusk

From far, Custer found a vague form
breaking the snow-plane. With the edge
of his hand & with his rifle,
he knocked crusts from it, stood back,
kept working to uncover it,

himself the artist of this beast,
a bull buffalo frozen into marble,
untouched by wolves, magnificent in power,
black horns polished to black gleam,
ice-shagged head a revelation,

hump & shoulders, flanks, tail
that broke in his hands. No matter:
he could not resurrect, could not start
that heart within that chestcage beating,
unless he could: he placed his lips

over its nostrils, but these were clogged;
he ran his bare hands over its side,
& found, & cut out, a long-buried arrowpoint.
For a moment, the creature shuddered, &, but no,
he'd only imagined. Even for an instant,

behemoth could not reawaken into its dream
of a thousand generations. Later,
Custer kept looking back at it until
dusk's red sunlight fell behind it
as though from one dead star onto another.

At Source

Sudden whiteout, the white so pure white
that even Custer's shut lids did not dim it,
or his white thought: why is the world not
always this white? what was to stop it?
Overwhelmingness of whiteness seemed implicit
in the nature of things, nothing to block it,
nothing at source to swallow the blanketing snow.

The Answer

Crying for a vision,
Crazy Horse stood on the skull
of a bull buffalo from dawn to dark,

facing the sun, no food or drink. His toes curled
into the eyesockets, but he heard
nothing, saw nothing,

so planted the skull
in the mud bottom of a river, &, all night,
stood on it, heart-deep in moving water & still stars:

at first, when his testicles shriveled & all thought condensed
until the buffalo's horns pierced
his belly, spine, skull,

he did not know that this was the vision
he'd cried for.

Disk Text

Crazy Horse tracked stories on the keyboard of his new machine.
On the screen, the past appeared: Bear bearing twins
on his starry back to another world,

Old Woman whose belly swelled with lakes & rivers,
Buffalo whose hoof flaked
Paha Sapa. . . .

Children looked over the Strange One's shoulder, seeing
nothing of what he typed except
themselves

in their own fragile,
miraculous life, running, wrestling,
gathering berries, as we, dreaming the dreamer from this far,

see ourselves
in the storied heavens. Crazy Horse knew
Lakota children would be forced to learn by way of these machines,

or die. Eternity
is now, but now other shapes, artificially
intelligent, herd on his screen, grazing relentlessly into the future.

Repast

Custer sipped soup made from buffalo fat
& berries mixed with buffalo blood,
& found it good.

He ate the soft nose gristle
mixed with marrow from the leg bones,
& found it good.

He ate the cheeselike intestinal content
of newborn calves killed in spring,
& found it good.

He ate a buffalo bull's raw testicle
sweet-scented in cream & bearberry leaves,
& found it good,

& he thought, given enough time,
he could eat a buffalo entire,
every hair, & its eyes,

hooves, every vein & bone, & then
begin again: given enough time,
he could eat the whole herd,

& every other animal, & insect,
& every other living thing
in the territory of the Dakotas.

The Ravens

Custer at evening in an Indian graveyard with its silent sleepers.
One scaffold had collapsed, a skeleton rested its head on the ground,
bone toes in the air. A woman's long black hair
streamed down through decaying poles. In various roosts, ravens
seemed to prophesy his living presence while, around the scaffolds,

prairie flowers suffused the soft light of their colors. This world
of glass beads, buffalo intestines, flowers & the sweet stink of skeletons,
is being written by these ravens, he thought, these sable divinities,
& his thought pleased him, & if his thought were not theirs,
he would write *them*, & thus come to be the keeper of the dead.

The Fossil

Atop a butte, Custer found the fossil of a sea turtle, all motion,
its vertebrae a curve of speed within
the split rock.

Now the only ocean was the wind's, its vast surround without surcease.
You could sometimes not hear yourself think,
as of this

fossil swimmer that once fed in waves where now God's breath
eroded rock. Custer wrapped his find
in a blanket,

tied it carefully to his saddlebag, & swam
upwind to the fort.

Rock Custer

Custer found a bear, larger than life, drawn on a rock
fifty feet above the plains, the yellowish-gray rock
not painted, the image not an infiltration of the rock.
He believed it a photograph taken by lightning
millennia before. That night, the prescient rock
flashed & seared with Ursa Major, & kindred Custer.

The Ancient Forest

In a Sioux medicine bundle Custer found a lump of coal.
In the coal, unseen except by us, the imprint of a fern.
That night, Custer lit edges of the coal with matches—
it glowed, but did not flame, but, unbeknownst to him,
inside the coal the fern-shaped air warmed until
its last spore woke in Mesozoic dark, & died.

The Fish

In a place where no white had ever been,
Custer rode with Bloody Knife to something
breaking the horizon. In time, they reached it,
a huge ovular stone. The scout signed
& grunted gibberish Custer could not fathom,
something, it might have been, about a fish
that once swam above these plains. Whether
the ancient creature resided in this stone,
or this was one of its eggs in petrification,
or this entity was the shape-shifter itself,
only Bloody Knife knew for sure. Nothing
Custer could figure made the story clearer,
though the Indian puffed his cheeks, performed
a breaststroke, & pointed upward.
No, it was no use. Custer remained obtuse,
& as he slept beside it, constellations winked
from the stone's shell, or forehead.

Except

Custer posed to himself the central question:
why is there something instead of nothing?
All should have been a black pure vacuum,
dreamless & wordless. The embodied life?—

absurd, illogical. Except that Libbie
could never not have been. Her spirit
must have existed at the beginning, implicit
in the nature of nature. All this exercise

of masculine thought—you could saddlebag it
where the sun don't shine or Libbie smile.
Still, how is there anything at all & not nothing? . . .
"Supper, Autie," she sang, calling him from his study.

The Holy

Custer, skimming,
happened upon Matthew 3:16,
Jesus's baptism:
"And lo, the heavens were opened up to him,
and he saw the spirit of God

descending like a dove, and lighting
upon him." . . .
What was going on?
Once, near Gettysburg, he'd seen a pigeon
counselling, or so it seemed,

a corpse, the bird
seeming to have the dead one's ear. Maybe
he himself had been privy
to the most holy possible moment, but was too
stupid to know it. Now, too,

he seemed to recall, in that forest gloom,
a supernatural light,
backlit wings, the unfortunate one's beard
haloed. The pigeon did
not panic, but lifted, easily & oddly

vertically unless, in his restlessness,
Custer were now just
kidding himself. Whatever to believe, he'd remember
to ask Libbie who herself was surely
a dove.

Custer Altamira

Custer was seldom tired, but now he was tired—
staring up at the cave's roof all night
by candlelight, wondering what to make
of figures painted there who knows when. . . .

Time to pack it up, return to his tent.
The buffalo & elk ignored him here to feed
on darkness. Abstracts of talon & feathery color,
the eagles disdained him here to fly.

He sat up, dizzy in the sputtering flame.
He found his rifle, & crawled toward the entrance
where his horse waited. His gloved hands
picked along the rocks. How long had that bear

roamed that sky ceiling? Well, no matter—
this would all be flooded, not without
his personal regret, but lost. At the Point,
he'd written a term-paper on the Red Man,

the necessary progress of civilization
to Christianize this chaos. Now that he'd
brainstormed among these animals, he'd
force his thoughts into order like a river.

Dildo

Custer, reading Highwater, realized he hated himself.
Like hell he did. What if all his soldiering,
all those charges into the rebs, his reputed honor,

were a kind of camp? He was no homo, no,
& the red writer had a point: tough guys acquire
a role to satisfy narcissistic desires

imposed on them. But screw all that. Let the next
afterlife, not this one, reveal the instrument
by which he might purge himself as by a pen.

Flame

Custer saw a maybe willow
spangled in yellow
as though on fire.
As he rode closer,
it kept wavering in flames.
Closer, & bits of flame
detached & reattached,
whole branches of flame.
Close enough,
& the tree seethed with butterflies,
aswarm, like bees,
in stirrings of first spring.
He reached his upturned palm
into them, gently—
they soon covered his arm,
& would have taken him completely,
but he brushed them back,
laughing. This was not
a tree filled with butterflies,

or butterflies in a tree, but
a tree butterfly,
a butterfly tree, one creature,
creation. This was Custer's
instant of flame.
He understood—
as you do, as I do,
briefly, but not
with that constancy
that could, possibly,
still save the world.

An Officer's Story

Custer cut a cutting from a dead Indian
& grafted it onto himself. "Look," he said,
standing there with his arms wide
as though that extra slip of carrion
attached to his chest were an orchard.

But the graft did take. We could see it swell,
day by day during the campaign until
he had to keep his shirt unbuttoned.
The tree, or whatever it was, branched out
up under his chin, & he was proud of every bud

but wondered aloud how long this could
continue. Then, one morning, he woke
with shadows in those limbs, hundreds
of cocoons, so went to work with shears,
reverting to his old self again.

Night Rain: The Sleepers

Each soldier had pulled his india-rubber hood
over his face. Custer, first awake, recollected
scenes during the war when, after a battle,
bodies of the slain were collected for burial.

Treaty

Said Custer, Here's how it's going down:
we'll ration water to the fish first come,
first served; grass to the buffalo by rank;
sky to the hawks one windgust at a time.
Keep your people quiet and in single file.
For any trouble, you'll sacrifice a child
a minute for as many of your moons
as ever bled your dirty women. Keep
questions to yourself, and call me friend.

Custer Describes His Mind

When I become engaged in a battle
and a great emergency arises,
everything that I ever heard or studied
focuses in my mind, as if the scene

lay under a magnifying glass. . . .
My mind works instantaneously but
always with everything I have known
brought to bear on the situation.

Hot Battle Cold Shower Custer

A comrade comments, "To Custer fighting and fornicating
are compatible. When he feels the need for a woman,
he leads a wild cavalry charge and stampedes
the old Adam out of his system."

Joe DeBarthe on Custer's Death

The friends and admirers of Custer
have nothing to regret in the knowledge
that the brave soldier opened the gateway to eternity
with his own right hand.

Meaning

One night as General George Armstrong Custer
whacked off in his tent on the Dakota plains,
at the moment of that first spurt of orgasm,
he heard something he'd never heard before,

a kind of plaintive inhuman voice, as though
in a single syllable an animal's thought
realized its own death, & spoke.
His cock wilted quickly, he folded

the handkerchief with its busy fluid
into a saddlebag, pulled on his pants & boots,
picked up a loaded pistol, & exited
to hear that ur-syllable again—poignant resonance

of yearning? of love? . . . No use, but
he remembered he'd seen its color,
which was ochre, a charred kiss of ochre,
the color of meaning & sound, this this.

Custer Receives His Name, 1868

The troops espied something glowing rising over lodges
of the Indian village. This was at first light,
on the Washita, before the attack. The object rose slowly,

almost imperceptibly, or could have been a rocket,
& continued its ascent, first appearing as flaming globe
of bright golden hue, then as purplescent being in the air. . . .

Rising higher, it grew larger, & moved more slowly, & its colors
changed from one to the other blended prismatic tint. . . .
One soldier exclaimed, "How long it hangs fire!" . . .

At last evolved the most beautiful morning star
any in the 7th had ever seen. Soon after,
Custer descended the slope to charge the village.

Past Manure Perfect

Soldiers rode in over the hill abloom beneath them—
pinks, magentas, lavenders, purples—pea flowers
that ripened into beans for drying for boiling

with berries & meat. Soldiers rode in over the hill,
their horses' iron hooves cutting vines
where the young had met their puberty dreams.

The Bride

After the 1868 slaughter on the Washita—
eleven warriors killed, & ninety-two squaws,
children, old men—Custer chose a white tipi
as his own souvenir, then ordered all other property

burned. Lieutenant Godfrey held in his hands
a bridal garment, "a one-piece dress adorned
with beadwork and elks' teeth on antelope skins
as soft as the finest broadcloth,"

& wanted to show it to Custer, to ask for it,
but thought to himself, "What's the use,
orders is orders," & threw it into the blaze.
For the rest of his life she kept him company.

Main Street Footnote

One of those murdered, shot in the back,
Chief Black Kettle was buried by his own people
in a beautiful hidden place until,

in 1934,

a crew of WPA laborers working on the Washita
unearthed him. *The Cheyenne Star*
displayed his bones & jewelry in a window.

After the Indian Camp Was Burned

One dog pulled a baby in a travois.
It ran from the fire, but ran back,
shaking the baby terribly.
Unable to catch the dog, the soldiers

shot at it, & it happened that the baby
received a ball. It was, perhaps, well
it was so killed, thought Custer:
if left behind, it would have starved,
or been eaten; if brought in,
he had no time to keep it or care for it;
dead, it was at least at rest.

Tick

As Custer burns a tick from Ginnie,
the smell of singed hair:
something he would rather not remember:
on the Washita, a squaw fell into a fire.
Her hair crackled, then burst. . . .

The tick is obscenely swollen,
its pilfered blood blue-green. . . .

When torched from outside, the tents flared;
from inside, they glowed before collapse.
The squaw's hair stank of burning grease,
her face smoked, he could not see her eyes. . . .
Ginnie's eyes thank him for this fire. . . .

Modesty: Custer to Elizabeth from Manhattan, 1871

Attended a dinner, opposite the poet Steadman
who sought for an introduction and told me
that during and since the war I had been to him,
and, he believed, to most people, the beau ideal

of the Chevalier Bayard, *knight sans peur
et sans reproche*, and that I stood unrivaled
as the young American hero. I repeat this
to you alone, as I know it will please you.

The Husband: Custer to Elizabeth from Manhattan, 1871

A beautiful young girl, eighteen or nineteen, blonde,
has walked past the hotel several times trying
to attract my attention. Twice for sport I followed her.

She turns and looks me square in the face,
to give me a chance to speak to her.
I have not done so yet. At her house she enters,

then appears at a window for any attention I may offer.
I called on Mrs. Hough. I told her about the young lady.
Mrs. Hough has the clearest, most ringing laugh.

Proverb

Since "a woman is the best dictionary," Custer,
ostensibly to learn the language of the Sioux,
bade to his bed a certain favored Meotzi who,
while coming as both interpreter & lexicographer,
tongued her primal word-horde into his ear.

Meotzi & Elizabeth

At the Washita, after the 1868 slaughter,
troops forced Cheyenne women. Custer
took beautiful Meotzi, who bore his child
whose hair showed pale streaks. Meotzi:
soon shunned, but squealing in his mind
with each future procurement of erection.

Beets: Custer to Elizabeth
from the Wichita Mountains, 1869

Tom & I sat on our horses as the view spread before us,
worthy the brush of a Church, a Bierstadt,
the structure of the mountains reminding one of Yosemite
in the blending of colors—sombre purple, deep blue,

to crimson tinged with gold . . . while the valley below
displayed a rich grass of a kind unknown to me,
varying in color from that of ripe wheat
to that of beet leaves and stem. . . .

Accountability

A thought occurred to future Custer,
before he lost it:
if buffalo bladders contained residue of the plains grasses,
of pooled rain & river water,
then oil terminal storage tanks, too, were bladders,
these containing essences

of ancient roses & pterodactyls. Buffalo piss
seeped into our brains,
rich with promise, but pterodactyl eyes brightened into
the eyes of Jesus. Therefore,
for whatever reason or reasons, the Indian must be held
accountable for whatever.

Wolverine

Custer underground—a wolverine's tunnel
big enough to walk in. Sudden thrusts—
horses' hooves puncturing his ceiling—
but he'd keep on, wouldn't he,
toward that determined destination.

The only light beamed from his helmet,
the beam moving when he moved his head.
He brushed through roots that wet his shirt
with stains of regret, but he kept on, didn't he,
to the edge of a cliff below which

a Sioux village waited, hundreds of tents
glowing from within, their cooking fires
revealing the flesh tones of the skins, warm
yellows & oranges & reds. Suddenly, behind him,
he felt the tunnel's inhabitant howling toward him.

Breasts

A dozen Indian women appear to Custer in a dream
in his tent he's cross-legged in buckskins it's
winter the women have snow on their backs & hair each
lays a cradleboard baby on his lap his lap

is filled with children the children seem made
of beadwork & horn the children are silent the children
are vortices of cold along his thighs belly chest
& the women are touching him with warming fingers & saying

our breasts our breasts our breasts our breasts contain
no milk we cannot feed our children there are
no berries the people are starving there is
no meat the people are crowding the scaffolds there is

no wood the living are cold he stands up with so much
to do in his tent an antelope a skunk to stuff
& specimens to pack for the eastern zoos the women
could fit in the next wagon of wooden boxes the children . . .

Taxidermist: Elizabeth Misreads One Word in a Letter from Her Husband, 1873

Often, after marching all day, long after the camp is asleep,
a light may be seen in my tent, and a looker-on might see me
with sleeves rolled above the elbow, busily engaged
preparing the head of some Indian killed in the chase.

The Gambler

Custer held in one hand six stones of the wild plum,
Sioux dice; in the other, dozens of silver earrings,
the integers of wager. I'm gambling
that I'll find you bastards, he thought,
& shook the dice onto his kitchen table,
as Libbie in her nightgown walked in on him.

Pennsylvania Avenue

Sometimes, in a no-win situation,
you can't win, but sometimes . . .
Custer raised his last half-eagle
into the biggest pot of the evening,
got called, got hammered.
Libbie was half-awake even before
she heard his boots hit the floor.
Again, she did what she could

to siphon his anger,
but he'd still, she knew,
berate himself the whole night through.

Those next days, he'd brush her hair
& swear, Libbie, with all his heart,
wouldn't he, but rascal Tom
& the other officers ragged him
who had no feel for the disciplined
mathematical intuition of the game,
& he'd join them again, until,
as with drinking & profanity,
he'd give it up, completely,
to bank on the Indians
for a lifetime's household money.

President Literacy

Custer found a squaw weaving cloth in a rude loom.
Through threads tied to sticks fastened to a frame,
she passed a string of beads, pressing the whole together
in the manner of a weaver.

He fingered a purse she'd made for a trader, the colors
of its beads arranged beautifully. Another purse
bore the beaded-legend, JAMES BUCHANAN. Custer
asked if she could read:

no, she said, but unwrapped for him a medal presented
an elder of the tribe by the Great Father in Washington—
from under the white chief's hard face she'd copied
this mysterious design.

The Twitch

Something kept twitching in a corner of his study.
Libbie had retired, Custer leaned over his desk
writing another essay for *The Galaxy*,
but something twitched in a corner of his study.

Forget it, but just when his reverie remembered
shooting his own horse dead during the pursuit
of a huge bull buffalo, whatever it was
in the corner of his study twitched again.

He hated to break concentration,
to lift his lantern to where the twitch
twitched, but did, finding the flotsam & jetsam
of the soldier's nomadic life, but no mouse,

scorpion, or plains spider that might siphon fat
from its sleeping human host. Nothing but boxes,
but, once he'd returned to his desk, the twitchy
twitch twitched again. Son-of-a-bitch.

Live Oaks, 1870

Custer dreamed he grazed with antelope, but not
under open prairie sky. Trees towered
dark as fairy tales, each with a door in its side.
Auratic grass & mushrooms exuded perfume,

Libbie's, & her gossamer hair swayed
in windblown patches in the cold air
of this autumn story through which he walked
on all fours, tasting. The animals thought him

one of them, helping to ground him here,
& their backs shone like gold blood in the leaves.
Behind those doors, the dead waited, & would,
for as long as he'd need. That war was over.

Officer Hours

Custer's favorite scout, Bloody Knife,
woke with a toothache, his jaw swollen.
Custer tied one end of string to the rotten chopper,
the other to his rifle. Keep your mouth open,

he ordered the Ree, who did, then
flung his rifle about ten feet at which point the tooth
leapt out. Bloody Knife's look was such
as inspired all to drunken imitation.

Elizabeth Considers Her Husband at Thirty-five

Carelessness in the wearing of his costume.
Troop boots to his knees.
Buckskin breeches fringed on the sides.
A dark navy blue shirt with broad collar.
A red necktie whose ends floated over his shoulder.
A broad felt hat, almost a sombrero,
on which was fastened a slight mark of his rank.

Nearly six feet in height,
one hundred and seventy pounds.
Deeply-set clear blue eyes.
His hair wavy and golden in tint.
His mustache tawny, complexion florid
except where his hat shaded his forehead,
for the sun always burned his skin ruthlessly. . . .

Hunting was generally with fox hounds
in the timber and underbrush along the river.
Almost constantly during the brutal winter
a saddle of venison hung in the woodhouse,
black-tailed deer to vary the monotony of beef.
What I wouldn't give to live that life again.
We made love as in a dream. . . .

The Meat

The three Custer brothers,
camping alone,
had hung a saddle of elk
high over their fire,
but wolves appeared,
drawn by their gravity
of smell, & these
were the *Kosh-e-nee*,
the dreaded timberwolf,
but the Custers woke, & did not
fear for themselves,
& rolled far from the coals
to watch. Presently,
one of the growlers
leapt for the warm
& dripping meat, but only reached it
with its nose, & fell,
scattering coals.
George shot it dead.
In five minutes,
another leapt.
Tom shot it dead.
The next was Boston's.
And so on.
They killed eight wolves
as that unreachable
luscious dripping meat
twisted
above the fire.
A ninth,
which they examined,
not yet dead,
its snout shot off,
lolled out its firelit tongue
& licked at the blood
from a companion's fur.
There were more wolves out there

than the brothers
had bullets,
but this night's sport
concluded in laughter
& wonder.

Elizabeth on Odorless Wildflowers

The gorgeousness of reds and oranges of prairie blossoms
surprised me. I had not dreamed that earth could so glow
with such tints. Spring rains had soaked ground long enough

to start into life the wonderful dyes that for a brief time
emblazon barren wilderness. The royal livery floats
but a short period over their domain,

for the cessation of even night dews, and the intensity
of scorching sun, shrivels the vivid, flaunting, feathery petals,
and burns venturesome roots down into the earth. . . .

What presumptuous things, to toss their pennants
over so inhospitable a land! But what relief, for travelers,
to see some tint besides the burnt umber and yellow ochre. . . .

Not one faint waft of perfume floated on the air about us,
and I remember starvation days of odorless life, when,
seeing rare colors, we expected rich odors,

but it was all we should have prayed for that such
brilliant heads appeared from such soil. . . .

Lakota Eye

When Elizabeth bit into the fruit brought her by Bloody Knife,
its consistency unsettled her. Beneath its fuzzy skin & firm flesh,
something gelid, a yoke of glue that stung her lips, slightly,

some dim memory of purple dragonfly honey dropped into her mouth
in a dream. Later, when she heard its name, Indian faces appeared
behind her pupils, & the Great Plains warped into wings & mandibles.

Elizabeth: The Shorning

The next morning after the fire, afraid,
I went to inspect our heaps of household,
a sorry collection—torn, wet, melted.

I lost silver and linen, what finery I had,
but the worst loss, irreplaceable,
I'd worn at a fancy-dress ball—

a wig made from the golden rings of curly hair
cut from my husband's head after the war. . . .

Lilies

Childless Libbie dreamed she bore a child
perfect in every way except
its head—what was it?—something
about its head, a pale horn growing
up from tendrils of cherubic hair
above its right ear, or was it the left,
or were there two horns, yes, two horns
the color of the ghost calla lilies
she knew as a girl & now curving toward her
larger by the hour. "What's the matter,"
Autie asked her when she woke,
but she could not remember. All day
this Easter day she thought of lilies.

Elizabeth Remembers the Trees

We transplanted cottonwood saplings from the river bank,
and watered them day in, day out,
and watched them struggle to survive. One day,
my husband called me to the door, and whispered me

to observe a bird perched on a branch,
enjoying the shade of two or three tiny leaflets.
Such a harbinger of hope had us looking forward
to days when our trees would cast a broad shadow.

The Jay

Libbie watched a jay in a tree over a grave
in the air. It thrust its angry posture forward,
& screeched. The platform below it seemed
to turn blue, & in her mind shadows flared

with blue edges. Black are the crow's caws,
she mused, blue are the jay's territorial cries.
Her husband seemed not to see the bird,
& climbed, as the jay blanketed the Indian sky.

The Wind

That year, a sirocco came up suddenly.
The sky became copper-colored,
stifling. The slightest touch of metal,
even door handles, blistered the fingers;

strong gusts shriveled the skin,
and burned grass down into the roots.
This wind lasted two hours, and we could not
restrain apprehension at the strange occurrence.

The White Disease: Testimony of Richard Irving Dodge

In going from one mountain pass to another,
we discovered an old Indian trail.
It was deep and wide, showed plain evidence
of frequent usage, but none of recent travel.
Winding along ridges for three or four miles,
it led by long and steep descent to a charming valley
nestled and hid in the very bosom of the mountains.
A beautiful stream wound in graceful curves
as if seeking to leave no spot of valley untouched
by its invigorating influence. Tall shapely trees
along the margins of the stream; greenest lawns
dotted with shrubbery, covered with lovely flowers
of every hue, made landscape fair as ever beheld. . . .

Descending the stream for some two miles,
we came upon the remains of an Indian camp.
Many of the old lodge poles were still standing,
though the lodges themselves had long decayed.
Scattered about were rusted and rotten cooking utensils,
arms, saddles, and in every direction
the dislocated skeletons of the Indian inhabitants,
some almost entire lying where the last
breath had left their bodies, others disrupted
and broken where dragged and gnawed by wolves.
To all appearance, nothing had been touched by man,
not a living soul had entered that camp since
the terrible days of visitation and dispersal.

Looney Tunes

Dressed in prized apparel,
a body in a tree:
blue army coat,
pair of tarnished epaulets,
& over its braided hair

parted in the middle,
a cavalry hat
with one feather
from the cock of the chaparral,
the road runner. . . .

Muse Food

This river moves past, slowly,
scummed with turds
from where the herd crossed
twenty miles away, three days before.
Among the turds, flies hum,
butterflies alight on surface tension,
lifting off if, as here, we so much
as think of them. This brownish
cyclical detritus of flowers & grasses
will float by for another day or three,
some eventually drying on the bank;
some pecked by birds, turtles, fish,
or dissipating until the water clears;
some reaching all the way to here.

Branches:

THE CAPTURE OF MOSCOW

Scout Frank Grouard Describes Crazy Horse, 1873

There were several young bucks there, he included.
Crazy Horse possessed somewhat unusual features.
He had sandy hair and a very light complexion.
He didn't have high Indian cheekbones, and didn't
talk much. He looked much younger than his age.
Powdermarks roughened one side of his visage.

Crazy Horse Tells Frank Grouard His Dream

He said he thought he stood upon some lofty height
and saw a mighty eagle soaring above him.
He watched it float in the quiet sky, but
presently it folded its wings and fell.
The eagle's body plunged to his feet,
and when he looked upon it, lo! it was himself.

Fishermen

Mari Sandoz wrote of Crazy Horse that he often tried
"to lift his mind to the land beyond this one."
In that here, in my experience, the words
but, but, but, but do not exist,
fat buffalo ribs do not roast over coals,
dripping linguistic juices. Here, for a time, spirit
drifts in allness like a net of smoke & earthcolors.

Brothers

When word came that Little Hawk had been killed by the whites,
the women in Crazy Horse's lodge made the keening, but softly,

& under blankets, for they knew that the Strange One, now
staring into darkness, detested this way of the people.

Beyond Culture

A warrior's shield must not
touch the ground, ever.
When his daughter fell against
its easel & knocked his over,

Crazy Horse did not laugh but spun
eons back in his brain
to where many-eyed dragonfly & thunderbird
hover. The child rubbed her shoulder

& ran to her mother for comfort.
Her mother was a deep crimsoning,
but her father replaced the symbolic thing
as though nothing had happened.

Richard Irving Dodge: Love Memoir

When I was a young man new to the plains,
with a heart full of romance and head storied
with Cooper's and other fictions of beautiful Indian maidens,
we were visited by a chief of the Northern Comanches
who brought with him a few warriors and his family,
several wives and one daughter, a vision of loveliness,
apparently about fourteen, but ripened
by the southern sun to perfect womanhood. . . .

Her form was slight and lithe, though rounded
into utmost symmetry. Her features were regular,
lips and teeth perfection, eyes black, bright and sparkling
with fun, and the whole countenance beaming

with good humor and bewitching coquetry.
A tightly-fitting tunic of the softest buckskin,
reaching halfway between the hip and the knee,
set off to admiration her rounded form. . . .

The bottom of the tunic was a continuous fringe
of thin buckskin strings,
from each of which dangled a little silver bell,
not larger than the cup of a small acorn.
Her lower limbs were encased in fringed leggings
and her little feet in beaded moccasins of elaborate pattern.
Her beautiful hair was plaited down her back,
and adorned with huge silver buckles. . . .

The part of her hair was carefully painted vermilion,
and a gold chain was twisted about her hair and neck.
What wonder, if with one look
I literally tumbled into love? She saw my admiration,
and with the innate coquetry of the sex in every clime
and of every people, met my eager glances
with a thousand winning airs and graces.
We could not speak, but love has a language of its own.

I haunted that Indian campfire.
Neither duty nor hunger could tear me away,
and it was only when the Indians retired for the night,
that I returned to my own tent and blankets
to toss and muse, and dream of this vision of paradise.
Next morning with the sun I was again with my fascination,
until one day she beckoned me to follow
into a glade, and I did, and there we came upon

several Indians standing around a slaughtered beef,
which was on its back, the stomach split open.
Taking up a knife, my maiden
plunged her lovely hand and rounded arm
into the bowels of the beast, found and cut off
some eight or ten feet of the gut, and, winding it
about her arm she stepped to one side,
gave the entrail a shake,

and inserted one end into her beautiful mouth.
Looking at me with ineffable content and happiness
expressed in her beaming countenance,
she slowly, and without apparent mastication,
swallowed the whole disgusting mess. . . .
I returned sadly to my tent, my idol shattered,
my love gone. I need hardly add that that
one Indian love-affair has satisfied my whole life.

Snowbirds

Custer saw snow dotted with bodies . . . birds
frozen to death a few days before . . . the squall
merciless against even indigenous creatures.
His Arikara scouts gathered bagfuls

for later plucking, a winter harvest, not unusual,
even expected: the Great Mystery possessed
invisible arrows numerous as snowflakes until
birds opened their eyes in the bellies of the people.

Snowblind

Curly watched a medicine man cure a woman.
The wise one sprinkled snow into her eyes,
sang a song his snowdream had given him, & blew
more snow onto the back of her head. Soon,

needles of light in her eyes melted,
Curly saw green shadows evolve in her irises.
Praise to the power that balances light, they said,
that focuses grass up through ice.

V

An arrow of geese passed over the village,
& then another. The children pointed,
waved their arms, clucked & honked,
then arrowed & ran out over the grass,

laughing. Crazy Horse closed his eyes:
up there, stretching his neck forward, his legs
tucked up under his belly, beating his wings,
he'd reach safety, sweeping his people behind him.

The Bead

He wondered where he was when he wondered
where he was. At such times, as words formed
relentlessly above & behind his eyes, he could
not touch, smell, or hear the here to which

a birdcall, or voice, or flapping flap
returned him. He had to laugh: the Great Mystery
was not a puzzle, but a stone bead
you sucked on to taste your own tongue.

Being Here

To unclench his mind: pine bough
springing back from melting snow.

Wildcat

Crazy Horse espied a wildcat in a hawk's nest
in a hollow tree, resting, its eyes drowsing halfway
open in dappled sunshine . . . closing . . . half opening. . . .

The human sat back against a boulder, untensed himself
. . . toes . . . abdomen . . . face . . . drowsed his eyes halfway
closed . . . open . . . closed . . . in dappled sunshine. . . .

Trance

He wanted nothing, except that, but what was it,
but no matter. When he fingered hailstones onto his chest,
his nipples filled & tightened. The Oglala language
sputtered a few last syllables behind his eyes,
& then that, but what was it, but no matter. . . .

Part of his horse as he rode, part of the air, invisible. . . .

Later, he remembered the riding toward, the arrival
wherein challenge-cries & death rattles
& the snortings of horses all threaded the shawl
of the Great Mystery of the single word of being, & he
wanted nothing, except that, but what of that other

part of it, the falling out of it? Because of that,

he would not celebrate with the others, would not
talk around the fire, describe, explain, boast,
but took himself away. Alone under the sky
of yellow wolf-howl & scents of green smoke,
this Crazy Horse, the Strange One, slept himself awake.

Good News

To learn their luck, the Minneconjou tied a blanket
over his head & sent out the half-man dreamer
who allowed his horse its trance, & followed,
& when he returned,
                              good news: more enemies
soon to die than the many claps of his hands.
They gave him presents, & Crazy Horse zig-
zagged to battle in his own black blanket of brain.

Ghosts

What some call *bliss*, some call *passion*, or *fire*.
Crazy Horse understood the whites' fires were out,
even their pilot lights had gone out:

the pale ones ran around smelling gas,
not knowing its sources or what must transpire
before their ancient inner forests could flame.

Pebble

No matter in this world or that, Crazy Horse reaches into a tree-
trunk at waterline, but cannot find the turtle,
but his fingers find a pebble

that shines bright white in the sun. The pebble is glad
to be above water, so sings; to be tasting
the green sunlight, so sings.

Such a small thing to be filled with so much song,
Crazy Horse thinks, & even this thought
causes the white pebble to sing

its joyful song. Where did you come from,
how did you happen to be here
beneath willow water,

he asks it, but it has no time for time. Its song overflows
the Strange One's chest with eternity,
with now.

Crazy Horse Nauseous

He knew he'd see
Lakota warriors
in army hire,

wearing blue coats.
In the sacred hills
he vomited blue bile

in which he read
the inevitable while
his horse danced crazy.

Paha Sapa

Crazy Horse slept digging a tunnel into the sacred hills.
He & we could dig it a long ways, a very long ways.
In the center of these hills, we'd begin the hollowing,
the long timelessness to complete this huge space
under the domes of the hills, but then the people could live:
surely, the Great Mystery will shine a sun over that withinness;

surely, grasses & flowers will grow, rivers course; surely,
when the people pray & dance, animals will find them
where miners cannot reach them. If soldiers dare

charge into the tunnel, buffalo will wedge it closed.
Let inhumans keep the outer world to themselves. . . .
Spoonfuls of tunnel into darkness into Lakota sleep. . . .

One World

At a small pond ringed by willows & twilight,
Crazy Horse, who had not slept for how many days,
stared into his face filled with frogspawn,
with stars. So, that was where the dead lived,
& waited, there behind his eyes. He'd never again

worry where he would spend eternity, this now, as long
as one Lakota lived to contain the world. . . .
His horse snuffled from its tether in the willows—
they'd return to the village, & fall awake,
& dream the stars in the pond, the spawn in the stars.

Bone & Velvet

In defense or warning, the bull elk emits a low whistle.
Custer heard in it the soft natural "E" of the organ,
& practiced the note himself until he could almost feel
in his forehead the first bulbous beginnings of horn.

Venison

An elk herd moved past Custer in the twilight,
gray silhouettes against snow & snow-shrouded pines.
He didn't know if they saw him there, moving

only his eyes. Were he to raise his rifle,
he & his officers would have venison for dinner,
but the herd moved past him, into the wood,

out of sight, while he'd been half asleep, while
evening deepened into a charred gray, while
he'd been thinking of nothing, & everything.

Discovery

Today, in this storm of crystals, every single one seemed
broken in half.

His horse's mane filled with intricate half-hexagons
thrown down by world's

original artificer: fathomless, relentless, inexhaustible,
inspired, oblivious,

thoughtless, capricious, excessive, you name it: from a silvery dust
to drifts ten times deeper

than this herd frozen in its canyon shelter. & maybe one
crystalline asymmetric for each star

in the blurry out-there. No, there ain't no making sense or order of it,
he said to no one.

Winter Mind

Custer had heard of a band of warriors painted absently white.
They rode white horses, their war dress consisted
of white cloth & white feathers. Poised
on a brow of hill, they seemed

boulders blanketed in snow. Eyes closed, he tried to delineate
their outlines as they waited above the 7th, but
his mind became a disk of all colors
spinning wildly white.

The Rock

Crazy Horse, on the sixth night, reached a wall of rock solid except
for six doors outlined in moonlight. Pressed his ear to the first,
heard voices of his own villagers; within the next, the earth-
trembling thunder of the herds; the third contained riverflow;

the fourth, birds of the plains & willowbanks; the fifth entered him
in images of tangled smoke, roots, scalps, dragonflies & horns;
the sixth, higher than the rest, seemed empty with such fullness
of the Great Mystery as he himself felt beating in his breast.

Cooper Institute, N.Y.C., 1870

Red Dog's speech, of which Crazy Horse had heard:
"When the Great Father first sent out men to our people,
I was poor and thin, but now I am large and fat.
So many liars have been sent out to us,
and I am stuffed full with their lies." . . . Yes,
Red Dog was the fattest Lakota Crazy Horse had known.
No, the whites' lies would not fatten everyone.

Microcosm

Grain of grit in his eye. Crazy Horse
pulled at the lash, pressed his forefinger
into the socket's corner, etcetera. No use:
the foreign object scratched when he blinked

or moved his eyeball. What next? Maybe
get someone to look close in case
a compacted hair or bit of fur or grass
stuck out. But it was more like sand,

& he could almost not remember when it didn't
enrage him. Otherwise, the day felt good,
but the eyegrit obsessed him again
with the whites, their persistence, their fort.

The Capture of Moscow

Western brain falls over the horizon.
Custer follows it with his, his
penchant for empirical romance:
"Libbie, the sunsets we see together
fuse our souls each to the other."
She sinks into his arms, their fort
pokes like a phallus into the darkness.

Faces

When Crazy Horse dug a hole & it filled with sky,
he knew that the center of the world was sky
filled with people who had lived before him,
& after him. The sky gushed out where-
ever it wanted, & when. Looking down,
he saw that his own face formed
from deep in this sky, & he was not surprised
to see himself seeing himself here.

When Custer dug a hole & it filled with water,
he knew that the water table was too high,
that this wouldn't be the best place
for a board floor unless the cavalry rigged up
a pump. His reflection seemed to weaken
& reminded him of dreamed scenes in which
thespians peered into mirrors,
shocked at how little life was left in them.

Trepidation

Custer wondered how his hounds
followed a trail in snow, rain, wind.
A grizzly stank, yes—urine & musk mixed
with essence of wildness—but only up close,
not over the distances the dogs slavered

in hot pursuit. What was in a smell,
what molecules clung even to pine needles
dry enough to burn from a bear's hot breath?
& what scent did he himself unconsciously
deposit with each step further into Indian country?

First Translation: The Warning

Custer unscrewed a white buffalo's horn from its skull
& found inside a message, written in signs on shell.
He nor his Ree scouts could read it, but we can:
"Long Hair, it's not too late, unless it is. Your woman
already grieves for you. Before either of us was born,
I waited, if it comes to this, but now place my words
in this hollowed horn of a white buffalo, just in case.
Yours in the Great Mystery. *Tasunke Witko.*"

Foreknowledge

One Custer artifact was a wooden bowl
from a burial platform.

Underneath was carved, entire, a bear. Claw-shaped incisions
shaped the lip.

Old, very old, a professor told him, old as anything of the kind
ever found above ground.

The bear looked over its left shoulder, right at Custer,
in fierce acknowledgment,

it seemed to him. Thus Custer wanted to fill the bowl
with bear blood,

& drink it in case, in that other place & time,
his totem had eaten him.

Circle

What emigrants called Devil's Tower
was the Bear Lodge of the Lakota, home
for that ferocious brother.

Custer imagined the earth level
with the top of that symbol
in the world before time

when spirit bears looked down to the plains
through erosions of eons,
knowing that Custer would come.

Bear & Cubs

The beast roared, fell, rolled over, got up, shook herself.
Custer snapped the exploded shell from his Henry,
raised the hammer, fired again, but she had moved, but, in luck,
he'd hit a cub who screamed her back to itself. Custer blasted
more bullets into her, but once more she broke toward her tormentor
who quickly put a ball into the second cub who also cried out.
Again, the mother returned to her young, Custer shot her again, again
she charged him, again he shot a cub to whom she returned. . . .

Later, he estimated he'd fired thirteen shots into her
before she'd retreated with her children into the canyon
where he found her pawing one of them: she turned it over,
as if to wake it, & shook it, & smelled its nose, & then
seemed to understand the fact of its death. She cried, cried
piteously, & stood up, making no attempt to charge him.
Ears flat, eyes blazing, neck stretched out, she howled, took
his last shot in her heart, rolled over, embraced a cub as she died.

The Bear

After midnight, after emptying the bearskull
& stuffing it with dry grass to dry it out,
Custer slept for his usual four hours.
This happened only once, but happened:
in dreamtime, below the moon, he padded
in the body of the bear, ravenous, confused,
carrying his own thoughts, in English, with him;
nevertheless, willow tangle & water shimmered,
he heard night sounds of the winged ones,
he moved through fern & canebreak that could as well,
he said to himself, have been Virginia wilderness
as here where Sioux slept with the bear
in their vision. He had to escape or outrun

their dreaming him, he knew, or he'd never waken.
He shook himself dark with green odors, his claws
clawed his face, he was crazed here, & then,
at last, he left the woods & found the two rails
gleaming across the land to the Indian village
where he would surely find, & kill, the dreamers.

Terror

High in heretofore unknown mountain fastnesses, Custer
pounced upon the ram bighorn from behind,
drew his knife across its throat,

but the old one's strength surprised him, it thrashed its horns
& almost broke his knee. Custer drove his knife
into one eye, then probed

for its heart, & found it, & sat down exhausted atop his kill. Then
he saw the ewe, fifty yards distant. Paralyzed,
she'd watched the death of her mate

in the grip of this strange & terrible animal.

The Swimmer

Libbie was tired enough to be two women,
both of them very tired. She dusted a little,
sat down, got up to rearrange some buds
in their crystal vase, sat down again. . . .

Life minus Autie fatigued her,
the rote work & worry. She felt like
just floating asleep for a month until
he'd be back to wake her. She'd feel

his mustache on her cheek, & roll over
on her belly, the way he liked her best—
his hands under her breasts,
her nipples between his gentle knuckles—

& hump up, lifting him with her strength,
drifting in wavedream, taking him in.

Tongue

A buffalo cow drank from a tub
in which Custer was dreaming a bath.
She didn't see him under the water,
must be. He watched her tongue
slip in & out of the waterline,
in & out. She left. He lifted up,
breaking staves with his erection.

Custer & Satanta's Son at Target Practice

Outside the camp, the two warriors
shot at buffalo skulls at various distances.
Custer always won, even when, just in case,
they exchanged rifles. At night, as always,
the dead buffalo gathered & circled,
with many more lives than they'd lived,
but each now in close range, & targeted.

Placefulness

Discipline in his camp, quiet, & sleep,
but far past midnight Custer woke to singing:
Little Robe, sitting against a tree,
oblivious to others, chanting an Indian melody. . . .

Later, pressed to explain, he said he'd been apart
from his lodge for too long, & the thought
of soon returning home had filled his heart
with gladness that could only be expressed in song.

Ropes

In camp, the coaches' tongues are turned inward—to these are tethered
the mules & oxen—
the cavalry wagons placed twenty or thirty feet apart, & long ropes
drawn through
the hind wheels, to which are picketed the horses.

The Planting

Each attached his horse by the halter-strap
to the hilt of his sabre,
then forced the sabre into the ground.

Events in Time

Along the Heart River, Dakota Territory, near
the Northern Pacific Engineers' camp,
three antelope are killed
by hailstones,

one worker brained & their stock stampeded
by the severity of the storm.
Custer dwells on this—
June 25, 1873—

& writes Libbie. Exactly three years from now,
Crazy Horse will paint hail
on his body & ride
for the kill.

Timefulness

It being necessary to reach the Platte, 65 miles distant, in one day,
the parched cavalry still wended its way
under the night's full moon.

For hours men, horses, & draught animals struggled & suffered.
Many dogs accompanying the command perished
of thirst & exhaustion.

All the while, from bluffs bordering the Platte valley,
Custer could see the river, near though far.
Later, with the first

mouthfuls of water, that metaphysical west, which had been
suspended, swelled in their cells again
like a future childhood. . . .

Drinking, Custer recalled an Indian grave, a platform
on which reposed, apparently, a chief's son.
Here was his bow & quiver

of steel-pointed arrows; also, a tomahawk, ceremonial knife,
red clay pipe & bag of tobacco, parcels
of sugar & bread,

powders of colored paints to protect himself in war, a lariat,
a saddle, a bridle, & a buckskin scalp pocket
dripping beads.

Scalp Lock

1.

Often a strip,
but stretched.

Curved, & then,
to heighten effect,

the skin portion
colored,

sometimes beaded.
Sometimes the hair

dyed,
golden, crimson.

In the tent
of Custer's dream,

scalps were voluminous, & white,
color of all colors,

the only color
he could remember.

2.

Dodge once saw in an Indian camp a "scalp" consisting of almost
the entire skin & hair of head, face, breast, & belly to the crotch.

Custer Writing the Dialect of Plainsman Comstock

"Injun fightin' is a trade all by itself,
and like any other bizness
a man has to know what he's about, or ef he don't
he can't make a livin at it."

Epaulets

Custer watched
a male redwing
pick up a dried
buffalo chip
with its feet,

fly up a few inches,
& turn it over,
& let it go,
& look for worms,
beetles, grubs & such

where it had lain.
My feathered friend,
he thought aloud,
we have much
in common.

Mixed Scatology Metaphor Etymological

You've heard the expression "Up shit's creek
without a paddle." The Republican River,
which spread four hundred miles eastward

out of Colorado Territory, was called, in Pawnee,
Kiraruta, Shit Creek, because the buffalo herds
fouled it. This must have been behind

Sherman's 1867 orders to Custer: "Clean out
that Augean stable of hostiles along the Republican."
Laxative or enema, Custer charged like diarrhea.

Custer Discovers Thermodynamics

We could charge and drive them wherever we encountered them,
but this only caused the redskins to appear in
increased numbers at some other
threatened point.

Letter to Elizabeth from the Black Hills,
August 2, 1874

In no public or private park have I ever seen
such a profuse display of flowers.
Every step of our march is amidst flowers
of the most exquisite colors & perfume.

So luxuriant in growth are they,
that men pluck them without dismounting.
Some belong to new or unclassified species.
I glance back at the column of cavalry

and behold men with bouquets in their hands,
the headgear of their horses decorated
with wreathes of flowers fit to crown a queen of May. . . .
I named this Floral Valley. . . . Goodnight, my Rosebud.

In This Dimension

On August 4, 1875, Crazy Horse, on a bluff
over the Tongue River, laid eyes on Custer,
"Long Hair" as they called him. Custer had paused
with his cavalry troop of eighty-five men

to wait for foot soldiers & wagons lagging behind.
Yes, that was the one, the thief. Crazy Horse stared,
but Custer, as is fitting, never in this life
laid eyes on the Strange One.

Custer, Bootless

Crazy Horse caught Custer asleep under a willow,
but did not shoot him, or cut his throat, or force him
to imitate a porcupine. What he did do was cut

the white balloon tied to the big toe
of Long Hair's left foot loose, & return with it
to his village to contemplate that soul.

Perspective

In Crazy Horse's shield painting,
one dragonfly hovers in distances among hills,
one close,
but both are the same size,
& for good reason:
however tiny the distant darter appears to the eye,
it is the same size as the one
near your face.
The sound & volume of their colors is the same, & those
faster-than-starlight wings.

Everybody knows this,
so who is talking about what when talking about the real?
Therefore, shove your western concept
of perspective
based on appearances, not attar of truth, where the sun
don't shine, & while you're at it,
take your time.

Medicine

Crazy Horse swept through the Sioux encampment
hearing hooves behind him increase
to the rumble of thunder until
a thousand warriors followed him as he streaked
toward the river.

After crossing, remembered one who was there,
"He was the bravest man I ever saw.
He rode closest to the soldiers,
yelling to his warriors. All the soldiers
shot at him,

but he was never hit." In the museum shield cover
attributed to him: blue, red, & yellow
medicine symbols including
the Thunderbird attended by two huge dragonflies:
on the day called

June 25, 1876, the 7th Cavalry must have felt
trapped in the blade wings
of dragonflies
through which their bullets passed
with no effect.

The Grave

Crazy Horse dreamed himself into the Black Hills
to dig for turnips, he thought, but out from mud
emerged Long Hair who sat there spitting gold,

p-tooey, until his throat & mouth cleared.
Crazy Horse paid no mind, but continued digging.
The other's face filled with winged beetles

who formed a mouth to say, "Dig it deep enough
for both of us." All turnips were gold, & inedible.
Then there was only himself, on a faraway scaffold.

Crazy Horse in Love

Seeing light flaring the edge of his shadow
on the rock wall, he asked himself,
"Why not become all flame?" As the sun fell,
that question kept searing him until,

that night, alone under the stars but asleep with her
her laughter her hair her legs her breasts
her face her buttocks, a flame shuddered from him
for the first time, like this, Crazy Horse in love.

Now

Black Buffalo Woman, now married to No Water,
now looked at Crazy Horse straight & open,
& teased him, & all could now see & hear.
He needed a wife, she said, & now Little Hawk,

Crazy Horse's brother, took up the theme.
Wouldn't a woman rather have himself
than the silent one? The women agreed,
& now laughed, & now the silent one

stared at the son of Black Buffalo Woman & No Water
in its cradleboard leaning against a saddle,
& now the silent one, inside himself, wept blood
from that old wound that now needed

to be sutured by solitude. Now, already,
he breathed shadows from the corner of the lodge,
far from the talkers as they talked
for a long time, until the child cried.

Black Buffalo Woman

Crazy Horse walked in the storm in only his breechcloth.
If he'd painted hailstones on his body, he'd be safe,
but lightning branched down around him, & he could smell it,
its yellow bitterness, acrid under his hair from this deep loneliness
for another's woman branching like black lightning inside him.

Riding Away with Black Buffalo Woman at Last

He in buckskin shirt & dark blue leggings,
his long braids wrapped in beaver fur,
one eagle feather behind his head.

She also in buckskin, & her hair braided
by Crazy Horse, & her cheek bearing
the vermilion circle of one deeply beloved.

Horns

Crazy Horse, shot in the face by No Water,
his jaw fractured, through the pain saw
so much light he thought himself blinded,
& would he ever see again? The bullet

exited. Something was finished with,
but what? Time to sleep for a long time,
& recover. What had the whites to do with this,
except everything? Black Buffalo Woman

ran from the tipi in one direction, No Water
in the other, but these would come together,
without himself. The light was such
of endless detached white horns in white sun.

Rods & Cones

A woman who loves Crazy Horse
cannot be with him.
This night again,

her husband done with her,
she receives that other,
the Strange One

who enters her who cannot
be with him.

Play

She can now sit up by herself.
Her father touches her nose
with a rabbit's foot
tied to a bowstring,

& now she is older, her braids
dancing as she rides
on his shoulders
as though he were a horse.

Rattle

Crazy Horse rattled a gourd rattle
filled with pebbles. Soon he could hear
the pebbles' voices, each different but all
singing the same song. Soon his own voice
joined those from the rattle. Soon he rose
to rattle this song among earth & stars
for as long as we live, or we're lost.

Willow

Crazy Horse returned from a war strike against the Crows.
In his village, friends had loosed their hair,
many had gashed their arms & legs,
for his daughter was dead.

They told him where. He travelled to a far edge of prairie
where her scaffold stood. Here are her playthings—
antelope hoof rattle, rawhide loop strung
with colored beads—

& here is his daughter, wrapped in a red blanket.
He leans against the scaffold for a long time.
He leans against the scaffold so long
the sun implodes

into its essence, so long . . . that he resembles a willow
growing above her, so long . . . the girl knows
he is rooted above her
to shade her.

Poison

Curly had once seen arrows poisoned,
the rattler pinned with a forked stick,
tickled the length of its body, angered,
a deer liver dangled before it, the rattler
striking the liver, sinking fangs into it
three, four, five times, then pinned again,
furious, unpinned to strike the liver again
that blackened & emitted a sour smell.
Arrows were thrust into it, withdrawn,
dried in the sun, a glistening scum adhering,
which, if it touched raw flesh, meant death.
Now, Crazy Horse would stuff that liver,
entire, into the white man's mouth.

Colors of Crazy Horse in Battle

White or yellowish hailstones dotting his body.
Skin of a red-backed hawk tied in his hair.
Blue lightning streaks on his cheeks.
Nose-bridge black.
Black eyes.

Seeing

Short Bull said Crazy Horse had black eyes that
hardly ever looked straight at
you, & missed
nothing.

The Eye

On this day that Crazy Horse rides out
into the rain, his paints wash down from him
onto his pony. The pony's fur blossoms
in these earthcolors, berrycolors, colors

of pumice & bone powders. Horse & rider
do not have a mirror except the rider's eye
in his loins that squints & seems
to laugh with him. Another good day to die.

Sacred Object

Crazy Horse's stone,
worn on a thong—
third planet flung
out from the sun.

Resolve, 1876

Custer watched blocks of ice unclog the river,
spring reaching even here. The Sioux,
as they had for centuries, would soon travois
their flimsy villages toward the migrating herds,

but this year something new in the equation,
he himself & his 7th. He'd corner the enemy
on their hunting grounds, & break them,
& run them in, without reservation.

The Ascent

Once, running a buffalo, Custer fired
& shot his own horse through the head,
leaving himself stranded out here

where anything can happen—
Sioux & Cheyenne,
rattler punctures & poison—

but from under his cavalry hat
he shook out
his long redgold hair & climbed it

in godspeed
to Little Bighorn where,
cut off, surrounded,

enswirled in chaos & noise & death,
his last thoughts ascended
to wife Elizabeth,

who, in her best-selling memoir
Boots and Saddles would write,
"In our plans for a home

in our old age, we included
a den for my husband. . . .
We had read somewhere

of one like that ascribed
to Victor Hugo. The room
was said not even

to have a staircase, but was entered
by a ladder which the owner
could draw up the aperture after him."

Bark:

POOL & PLACE DATA

The Stage Stations

all had dugouts as retreats
in case of flaming arrows:

four-feet deep, a roof of timbers
bearing several feet of earth;

loop-holes left under the roof-beams
for egress of rifle fire, as here.

BIA

The men in the cabin had dug a cellar
and tunneled to the bank of the river
and could pass out from cabin to river
without being seen.

Eighteen of us went with the help-seeker
and rowed up the river under the bank
so the attacking Indians could not see us.
We got into the cabin

before daybreak, over twenty of us in there.
When the savages attacked, we killed eleven,
then unbarred the door and ran off their brethren
of paint and feather.

Rock & Roll

Soon after falling into the coach,
the dying soldier had breathed his last,
but for five miles his dead body kept
slipping from its seat onto the prostrate woman.
In vain, she pushed it to one side; the violence

with which the vehicle rocked in ruts
as the driver urged his mules to utmost speed,
kept it hard for her to keep herself
from contact with the corpse that rolled
with the plunging of the coach.

The Wheel

The leg of a horse is wedged in a wheel
of a coach under attack for six hours.
No one can safely get to it to amputate,
not with arrows & bullets flying. Nothing
to do but wait it out, at least until dark, when
maybe the wheel can be freed. . . .

Ars Poetica

The wounded soldier suffered much,
        his only relief being in a constant change of horses,
        the different gaits
                of the animals furnishing change, if not
        cessation of pain.

White Place Names

In 1876 a writer in *Scribner's* asks,
"Surrounded by places whose names
derive from scenes of innocent blood,
do we wonder these frontiersmen
hate Indians with implacable hatred?"

Zygote

The fulcrum phrase in Custer's *My Life on the Plains*
occurs just before his Tabular Statement of Murders,
Outrages, Robberies, and Depredations Committed by Indians
in the Department of the Missouri and Northern Texas in 1868.
He refers to the Indians as the whites' "hereditary enemies."

Dodge on Deposition

The tenacity of life of an Indian is most remarkable.
He will carry off as much lead as a buffalo bull,
and to drop him in his tracks the bullet
must reach the brain, the spine, or the heart.

Incident

During the conflict at the place now called Beecher's Island,
an Indian boy shot an arrow into Herrington's forehead.
The scout couldn't pull it out. A companion cut the shaft,
leaving the iron arrowhead lodged in Herrington's frontal bone,
but then a bullet struck the object, & the two fell to the ground,
fused. After much laughter & cussing, then wrapping
a cloth around his head, Herrington continued fighting.

Exclamation Mark

A lone soldier had killed nine Sioux
        before being himself rushed & killed.
                The Indians cut nine gashes into the back,
                        one for each warrior dead, & stabbed the corpse
                nine more times. Next, they drove a stake
        into an eye, pulled it out, filled the hole
with powder, & blew the skull to bits.

Sitting Bull's Reply to a Summons, 1875

Are you the great God who made me,
or was it the great God who made me who sent you?
If *He* asks me to come see *Him*, I will go,
but the Big Chief of the white men must come see Me.

I will not go to the reservation. I have
no land to sell. There is plenty of game for us.
We have enough ammunition. We do
not want any white men here.

Downwind

To support the barrels of their heavy guns,
the whites drove forked sticks into the ground.
The whole herd dead, they drove stakes through noses
& pulled hides off with horses, leaving the rest,
even humps & tongues, for wolves & maggots.

Super Collider

The hunters did not realize, so in 1844 outfitted again—
larger wagons, better ammo, longer-barreled guns—
& moved north to the grazing grounds. *Nada.*
They assured one another,

& moved west for months,
each day expecting to find them. *Nada.*
At last, they accepted the worst: the herds were gone.
Broke, the hunters switched majors, & moved on.

Tongues

Buffalo tongues were pickled in salt, freightcars of them, &
shipped east in a rhythmic industrial music of the mind, millions of
tongues passing over our horizontal sleepers, clackety clack.

I don't know whether they were packed in wooden crates or barrels,
or if merchants supplied the hunters & shippers with stoneware vats,
the 20 & 50 & 100 galloners that still show up at country auctions. It
must have been very dark & very silent inside a vat of tongues.

But I'm wondering, to begin with, how hard it was to cut the
tongue out. How rigid were the jaws of the dead animal? Could a right-
handed hunter hold down the lower jaw with his right knee while
inserting the fingers of his left hand in the nostrils & pulling open the
jaws? In this way his right hand would be free to work a knife. But he'd
need two hands to cut out the wet tongue, wouldn't he? Maybe it had
to be a two-man operation.

They did not have to break out teeth to get to that organ, I'd guess,
but how far back did they make their cut? Did they try to get as much
root as possible, maybe a little palate, & was the root a darker or fattier
meat that chefs were glad to receive?

It must have been arm-wearying work to collect hundreds, thou-
sands, hundreds of thousands of tongues. Were they thrown into salt or
a brine solution right away, or put in leather or canvas bags, or Indian
baskets, or were they thrown onto a wagon? How much did one weigh?
I've read that in the buffalo killers' camps conditions were such that

skinning knives also "did duty at the platter," but just how big & what shape was the tongue-knife? Did much blood run from a tongue when it was cut? What colors was the tongue? Was it brown tending toward pink at the edges? Could you see mauve in it, as you can in the leaf of the broad-leafed milkweed still growing in prairie margins? Was there a white froth on it, & did its colors, later, change much? Could you judge its freshness by its colors?

In essence, tongues were made of the grasses & fresh waters of the plains, but did they have, when fresh, any odor—chewed grass mixed with saliva? dusty fur & urine & cottonwood bark? licorice pumice?

I've read that sheep & cattle eat grass to its roots, but buffalo ate only the tender upper shoots & allowed the plains to hold water against floods & to regenerate the grasses & themselves. Did their tongues, therefore, taste juicier & create in you thoughts of mysterious cyclical benevolence as you chewed?

Some of the buffalo must still have been half-alive when their tongues were cut out, & some must still have had beating hearts afterwards. Was the severance a surgical operation, a deft excision, or was the tongue hacked out? What was its texture? Was it smooth to the eye & touch, or was it surprisingly rough like the surface of coral or a bed of bluet anemones? Could you see the taste buds? Could you see the saliva ducts? Was the tongue bifurcated underneath like a heart? When you tried to pull it out, did attaching muscles cling to it like the chalazae of an egg or the tough strands that fasten a bivalve's body to its shell?

Did the tongue quiver when removed as though it were still trying to lap water? Did it swell quickly, or did it seem to lose bulk in the air? Did any of the hunters eat tongue raw as some people today eat special cuts of beef? Were tongues that should have been passed over ever harvested from decrepit or diseased animals? Were some tongues ulcerated or pocked with sores?

I've read various estimates of the number of buffalo that lived on the plains before the white onslaught. 30–60,000,000. By 1888 maybe a thousand survived. Today, the gene-pool must be dangerously shallow, only a glaze now after those millions of years of thunder & rain.

In summer, the killing & cutting must have been work engulfed in bloodsmell & flies; in winter, clumsy work with gloves pushing through ice-shagged fur.

We know that a hunter could shoot one animal & the others would stay with it & with one another until the whole herd was dead except for the bawling calves that were not worthy of or did not require bullets.

Did the hunters generally let these calves be, or did they cut their throats & take their tongues as special delicacies?

I'm sure the hunters were not sentimentalists & didn't spend any time staring into eyes, but were the animals' eyes usually open or closed when their tongues were taken? When the animals fell, did they sometimes bite off the tips of their own tongues?

Were the tongues of the bulls different in other ways than weight from those of the cows? Did the animals groom one another with their tongues? Did the buffalo sleep standing or lying down, & when they slept, did the tongue hang from the open mouth, or did it press against the back of the upper teeth in a moderate vacuum to keep it from obstructing the passage of air? Was the tongue useful for cutting grass as the animals browsed, or did it instinctively remain back in the mouth out of the way of the teeth? Did buffalo snore?

Just how tough was the tongue? Did it thwack through thorns & blade-sided grasses? Did a chef have to tenderize it with a mallet to break down its musculature before cooking? Was it a meat that could fry or broil in its own fats, or did you need lots of butter to keep it from sticking to iron? Before one of their debates, Abraham Lincoln & Stephen Douglas feasted on buffalo tongue. Did Edgar Allan, Emily, or Walt ever taste it?

Did tongue dry well for jerky? Were bits of it sprinkled on salads? Were tongues stuffed with vegetables & crabmeat?

I've read that in an eastern city you could buy a passenger pigeon for a penny. How much for a pound of hickory- or oak-smoked tongue, which had to come from further away? In the cities, was buffalo tongue a curiosity, something like alligator or bear or beefalo meat today, or did it become for a decade or two usual fare, even a staple? I can almost hear the butcher saying, "Here ya are, Mrs. Newlyn, a beautiful cut," can almost hear the merchants & houseboys & cooks slapping the heavy slabs of tongue onto wood counters & into drysinks.

Do you know the Georgia O'Keeffe painting of a steerskull twined with roses afloat in blue sky over a barren landscape? In place of that skull I see in my mind's eye a flayed-out buffalo tongue.

Long slices of tongue were sometimes dipped in batter & fried, or grilled, or baked, & chunks were stirred into stews, & there were choice steaks ordered rare or medium or well-done & served with dark American beers & French wines. Diners at first must have pictured the animals as they ate, but then the meat must have become the usual blur of habit.

Did your own tongue, when it contacted & manipulated that other tongue in your mouth . . . I can't seem to frame the question.

What was a tongue's consistency when you chewed? Did flavor & consistency depend on the time of year the buffalo were killed & the lushness of the plains' seasonal grasses, or did the buffalo, except in winter, always manage to keep pace with the ramifying growth? Did a winter tongue possess a winter tang?

Was there a difference between the taste of the tongues of buffalo for centuries Indian-run off ravines & free-fallen in dream-panicky air, & buffalo shot businesslike & dropped instantaneously dead from a distance? Does fear become taste?

Suppose a big kill, the tongues removed, the hunters gone back to camp or saloon. Full moon above the thousand carcasses where they fell. Wolves that had heard gunfire & come from twenty miles around & waited for dusk when the dead herd would be left to them. Did the wolves eat the humps or flesh sides & ribs first, or go for the viscera, & maybe the liver? Maybe the buffaloes' lips. Living snout to dead snout. Living wolf cubs playing & learning among the dead buffalo. In summer, how many days of eating before the meat was too rancid & maggot-ridden for the wolves, eagles, crows, rats?

In that other life of ours we might, in 1850 say, have bought a steak at our butcher's, taken it home, unwrapped it from the waxed paper moist with reddish salt, & cut thin pieces from it to fry in our skillet with butter & leeks, our own tongues watering for the wild buffalo of the plains that would soon enter our bloodstreams in Philly or New York.

Heat

In city sweat shops,
machines running with belts cut
from summer hides.

Testimony: Private Charles Windolf

You felt like somebody.
You rode a good horse,
with a carbine dangling
from the leather ring socket
on your McClellan saddle,
a Colt army revolver
strapped on your hip,
and a hundred rounds of ammo
in your belt and saddle pockets.
You were a cavalryman
of the Seventh Regiment,
a proud outfit
with a fighting reputation,
and you were ready.

Elizabeth: The Sharpening

Then, the sabre was more in use than later,
and it seemed to me that I could never again
shut my ears to the sound of the grindstone.

Belden on the Poisoned Arrow

This deadly weapon is made like other arrows,
except it has a poisoned point.
For years past, in wars along the Platte,
on the upper Missouri, and in all our contests
with the Indians, not a single soldier or citizen
has been shot with a poisoned arrow. Civilization
can never be sufficiently grateful, even to savages,
for having discarded a practice so barbarous.

Elizabeth Describes Gatling's Gun

a small cannon
discharged by turning
a crank that scatters
the shot in all
directions and is
especially serviceable
at close range

George E. Hyde on Agrarian Progress in Nebraska

". . . the placid sugar beet
having replaced the wild Oglala
as the principal feature
of the landscape."

The Big-Horn

A trader asked how to make a beautiful big-horn spoon.
An Indian advised, "First you catch the big-horn."

Job

I liked picking up the skulls best.
I could fling a calf's by one horn
maybe twenty feet into the wagon.
It didn't matter if it busted—
in fact, the smaller pieces the better.
But a bull's skull took two of us
to twist it off its stem and lift it.
You each grabbed a horn,

or did it the smart way with a pole
through the jaw and an eyesocket.
All in all, it was good work,
but ran out, but you had the feeling
of clearing something up, a job
no one would need to do again.

God Does Not Plow

is what a rancher
screamed at a farmer
whose blowing soil
buried grazing land
up to the fencetops.

Red Cloud's Demands, 1875

For seven generations to come,
I want the government to give us
Texas steers for our meat.
I want the government to issue
flour, coffee and tea,
and bacon of the best kind,
and shelled corn, and beans,
and rice, and salaratus, and tobacco,
and dried apples, and salt and pepper
for the old people. I want a wagon—
with a span of horses and six yoke
of work cattle for each family.
I want a sow and a boar,
a cow and a bull, and a sheep
and a ram, and a hen and a cock
for each family. I am an Indian,
but you try to make me a white man.
I want some white men's houses

built at this agency for the Indians—
nice, black shiny furniture, dishes,
and a scythe, and a mowing machine,
and a sawmill. If you want me
to be a white man, pay the bill.

Bourke: The Rattlesnake

This lovely country was abandoned to the thriftless savage,
the buffalo, and the rattlesnake; we could see the last-named
winding along through tall grass, rattling defiance as it sneaked away.

The Frontier

Crazy Horse, imagine this: all night in my lodge a tall box that keeps
                meat cool
hums, & a light with numbers shines American time from a machine
        in which invisible fire concentrates to cook.
        I don't know where such energy

originates, but not here in my brain & under breastbone where the
                Great Mystery
snores. I might object, & did not choose this tribe, this village, this
        country, except I guess I do, each day. Imagine: in winter,
        woodless fire & ripe fruit from west of where-

        ever it is your bones diffuse.

Triple Helix

Custer thought evolution a ladder, but he was wrong:
dogs evolved from wolves, *e.g.*, but wolves survive.
Evolution bushes like rhododendron, blooms petalling,
holding on in all shades of mauve dilapidation or maybe
perfect symmetry, survival simply of plants that survive.
Therefore, this Crazy Horse—DNA from one hair
with impeccable provenance, wedded to one of Libbie's,
ditto. She always didn't want a child, or did she?
Now this 21st century: by luck, guile, hoped-for beauty,
less bush than the mapped promise of algeny.

June 25, 1876

As Custer fell, he killed a man,
& laughed, Sitting Bull said.
Custer laughed as he died.

About 265 cavalrymen slaughtered
by thousands of Sioux & Cheyenne.
Custer, last in his West Point class,

enjoyed the noise & smoke & blood,
this crazy bastard of the plains,
much crazier than Crazy Horse,

first to fly at Custer across the river,
who knew, after this victory,
that he & all native peoples

would be driven over a cliff,
& it wasn't funny, but both knew who,
in the long run, would be better off.

December 29, 1890

Many Sioux men massacred at Wounded Knee
wore their magic white ghost shirts
whose force fields were solved
by white bullets.

Those Who Lived Before

Thirty-six years after the murder of Crazy Horse,
Fools Crow, who, born in a reservation district
near Wounded Knee in 1890 & who became a holy man,
saw a living buffalo for the first time.

This was 1913. He was on a train to Salt Lake City,
home of the Mormons. The train slowed near a place where
a white man kept eight buffalo, & was feeding them.
Fools Crow closed his eyes, & was struck into transport

to that world of those who had lived before.
Fifty years later he said, "I wish for my people's sake
that hundreds were immersed in constant vision-seeking
and prayer, but I am one of the very few left."

Semicolon Gene Calves: Pool & Place Data

In 1876 occurred the last sighting
of a substantial buffalo herd
within what became Oklahoma;

in 1883 two Oklahoma Panhandle ranchers
caught & raised a pair
of buffalo calves,

then decided to donate both animals
to their old home-town,
Keokuk, Iowa;

offspring of the Keokuk pair
became mascots of the Page Woven Wire Fence Company
of Adrian, Michigan—

"a fence that will stop
a buffalo will stop
any farm animal";

in 1904 the New York Zoological Society
bought four of the Page Company herd
& shipped them to Manhattan;

in 1905 President Theodore Roosevelt
(who in his pre-Roughrider twenties
hunted buffalo in the Dakotas)

declared the Wichita Mountains' 59,000 acres
a national game reserve;
in 1907 Zoological Society officials

shipped fifteen of its specimen herd
back to Oklahoma
to stock the new refuge;

by 1956 a thousand buffalo lived
at the Wichita Mountain site,
with others of the herd

sent from time to time
to American & European zoos; in 1930
the herd numbered about 500.

Tigers

To my right, in a showroom window, Al Capone's
bulletproof black limo, 1931. In front,
huge above The Strip, blonde Dolly Parton,
her teeth the shape & size of tombstones

on Custer's Hill. Across the street,
the splendor of Caesar's Palace & The Mirage where
white tigers perform their air-conditioned dream,
then rest their heads on pink marble. . . .

His cul-de-sac an easy day's ride from here,
I'd been reading Son of the Morning Star.
"O glorious war," he writes—all that chaotic splendor
of feathers & blood. . . . O Vegas, when, in a trance

of bonging slots I prowl your crowded aisles, I scent
our delicious craps & blackjack death-to-come,
never mind that old desire to dream alone
in a cave of shades in the Himalayas.

Human Interest

There's a call-in service in Vegas called Strippers Elite.
Megastar Cher was reported romancing a 23-year-old hunk
who works for the service. Ralph Petillo, owner & editor
of *Las Vegas After Dark*, was thrilled to scoop other publications:
"This is big news," said Ralph. "Only in Vegas can you see
this type of human interest story. Vegas is a great town."

When Cher was working The Mirage late last year
a friend of hers called Strippers Elite & had Eddie Romeo
sent to perform at a party in Cher's honor. According to Judy Sales,
Eddie's former girlfriend, they've been dating ever since.
"Cher stole my man," Julie says. "He's had his head turned
by all her fame and money. How can I compete with Cher?"

Julie told the *National Enquirer* she followed Eddie
to the El Rancho Bowling Alley where he first met Cher.
She saw them smooching, & left, sick-at-heart, but later
Eddie told her it was "just business." But it wasn't:
according to the *Enquirer*, Vinnie Milano, Eddie's best friend
& fellow Strippers Elite dancer confirmed the romance

between the hunk & the superstar. Says Vinnie,
"I saw Cher with Eddie the week she was appearing
at The Mirage in December. He was seeing her every night."
Also, other sources say the romance continued long after
the bowling alley incident. Julie's girlfriend Kim Cohen
said she saw the two in Cleopatra's Barge at Caesar's Palace.

Vinnie confessed that the couple has been getting together
at least two or three times a week when she's in Vegas.
"When she's in L.A. or Denver he sees her on weekends,"
admitted Vinnie, who further revealed that at one time
in the beginning of their relationship Cher dropped Eddie off
at his apartment when Julie happened to be there:

seeing Eddie exit the huge limo, Julie became distraught:
"My heart sank as the window rolled down
and I saw my boyfriend kissing Cher," sobbed Julie.
"When he got upstairs we had a huge fight.
Eddie finally told me it was nothing, that Cher
was 'just a friend,' but since then Julie has uncovered

scads of evidence that proves her man & Cher
are more than friends. Julie told of a gold bracelet
engraved "Love, Cher" that she found in Eddie's closet,
& a letter. What was in the letter she didn't say.
Eddie told Julie he's free to see whomever he pleases.
"I don't see what she sees in you," Julie told Eddie,

but also added she didn't see what Eddie sees in Cher—
"She's old enough to be your mother, Eddie."
Eddie told Julie that Cher finds him exciting,
a young & sexy stripper. She loves his long hair,
& Cher has a magnetic personality. She's fascinating,
says Eddie, who recently granted this reporter an interview:

Eddie says he hasn't been seeing Cher for a while now.
This was not of his own choosing. He wants Cher to know
he'll take her back on her terms. "I've never met someone
as wonderful as Cher," Eddie confides. Basically,
she got too busy for me and hasn't returned my calls.
I have many girlfriends, but would trade them all

for another romantic interlude with Cher. She's every-
thing that I could hope for in a woman." . . . Well,
Eddie's still as exciting to the girls as Cher is to him.
If you want to catch his act, & like feathers & guns,
you can call Strippers Elite at 625–1876. Inquire about
"Custer" & "Crazy Horse," Eddie's two stage names.

Dr. McGillicuddy on Crazy Horse

In him everything was made second to patriotism
and love for his people. Modest, fearless, a mystic,
a believer in destiny, and much of a recluse,
he was held in veneration and admiration
by younger warriors who would follow him
anywhere. I could not but regard him
the greatest leader of his people in modern times.

Cradleboard

Its mother reached the child to Chief Crazy Horse.
He caressed its head, plumped its fat cheeks.
"Little one," he said, "care for the old, the helpless."
The proud mother lowered her eyes in his presence,

& bent for her child. Crazy Horse returned
to his food, dried berries & buffalo meat. . . .
The child's grandson died in an alley in Newark,
that dim family story frozen in his vomit.

Quasar

Red Feather helped undress the wounded Crazy Horse.
In 1930, he said that for a time young Red Feather,
his son, had the stone Crazy Horse wore under
his left arm, a white stone with a hole through it.
Crazy Horse wore it in battle on a thong slung

over his shoulder. Yes, young Red Feather had it.
No, Crazy Horse was not wearing it when stabbed.
Yes, as others had also said, Chips, a friend,
gave the stone to Crazy Horse, who had been wounded
before wearing this gift, but never afterward

until his death when, at Fort Robinson for peace,
he'd been betrayed. Maybe, at the moment he died,
the white stone condensed into a black star
that fell through earth to now where
Crazy Horse is buried, no one knows for sure.

Short Bull on Photographs of Crazy Horse, 1930

I've seen two photographs that show him on horseback.
One shows him on a buckskin, one on a roan. . . .
I've seen a third photograph I am sure was him
because it showed him on the pinto he rode in the Custer fight—
I could not possibly mistake that horse, and nobody
rode it but Crazy Horse. . . . The man who owns these pictures
got them from soldiers once quartered at Fort Robinson.
He has a big collection. He lives in California now,
near the National Park. I do not remember his name.

The Steadying

Where we are, & at what speed: I know
we're spinning 14 miles a minute around the axis
of the earth; 1080 miles a minute in orbit
around our sun; 700 miles a second
straight out toward the constellation Virgo,
& now Custer is charging maybe a half-
mile a minute into an Indian village; but
from many eye-witnesses we know
Crazy Horse dismounted to fire his gun.
He steadied himself, & did not waste ammo.

Where we are, & at what speed: I saw
on display at Ford's Theatre in Washington, D.C.,
the black boots & tophat Lincoln wore that night;
at Auschwitz, a pile of thousands of eyeglasses also
behind glass to slow their disintegration;
in a Toronto museum, ancient mummies, ditto;
in Waikiki, some glittering duds once worn by Elvis; but
from many eye-witnesses we know
Crazy Horse dismounted to fire his gun.
He steadied himself, & did not waste ammo.

Where we are, & at what speed: I remember,
in Montana, a tumbleweed striking the back of my knees;
when I was a boy, a flock of blackbirds & starlings
beating past Nesconset for the whole morning;
at Westminster Abbey, in the stone corner, a poet's rose
for just a second drinking a streak of snow;
cattlecars of redwoods vowelling to gotham in my dream; but
from many eye-witnesses we know
Crazy Horse dismounted to fire his gun.
He steadied himself, & did not waste ammo.

Restoration: Alfalfa Woodstock 1994

A TV reporter, as his camera panned the devastation, said
"It looks like the Custer battlefield out there,
all that smoke and debris."

The music had died away in the early morning hours
from these hillsides of rain & mud,
condoms, shredded tents

in colors of hippie dreams, enough mega- & meta-garbage
as could fuel a dissertation.
What tonnage?—

the clean-up boss couldn't begin to speculate, but figured
they'd be on the job for at least six weeks
before the sowing of seed.

A Context for Riffs

Without that, all is askant or willy-nilly.
With it, splinteriest thoughts in sound cohere,
at least where it matters, where
subtext might satisfy: flies crawling

into the nostrils of the summer herd;
Libbie back at the fort polishing a silver salver;
Custer in his tent stuffing a wildcat;
Crazy Horse reaching in half-dark for his daughter.

Belden on Civilization

So it has been for more than 200 years: civilization touches barbarism,
and barbarism recoils like a burnt child from fire, and a voice cries,
'Back, back to the setting sun. I want your land, your game, your home,
even the graves of your people; and I will have all! all!'

Charades at Fort Abraham Lincoln, 1874

Pulled from a crystal bowl, the phrase was "Red Nigger."
Tom Custer held a feather-hand behind his head
& made a hideous face, turning his lower lip over
& placing his tongue upward over his upper.

Guesses came fast: "Indians," "medicine man," "Sioux,"
"heathen," "Bloody Knife," "Sitting Bull," "Cheyenne."
Tom bent over & leered & pantomimed wiping his private parts
despite the presence of ladies—"hostiles," "squaw"—

& then somebody got it. Most laughed. George thought it
in bad taste, but smiled, & went to the bowl, & drew
a phrase he thought he could handle, if he were willing
to make a goddamned fool of himself: "Crazy Horse."

Recommendation of the Commissioner
of Indian Affairs, 1877

The blanket must give way.
Garments should consist of coat and pantaloons, the coat to be
in shape like the old fringed rifle-coat or blouse,
belted at the waist,

our object being to secure both
comfort and uniformity, so that competitors for contracts might know
precisely what garments would be wanted
for Indian service.

Leaves of Horse

In 1877, the year Crazy Horse was murdered,
passenger pigeons still nested in great flocks
in the valley of the Ohio. In Brooklyn,
vendors served chestnuts from steaming carts.

That warrior is dead. The last passenger pigeon
died in a zoo in Cincy in 1913.
Chestnut trees were about wiped out by the '30s,
but here, among these leaves, a horse dances crazy.

Brackets

One of the 7th accidentally shot himself.
Custer sat right opposite when it happened.
The man let his gun fall, it turned over & hit a rock,
the bullet entered the calf of his right leg.

The next morning, delirious as the man was,
Custer could not send him back to the fort
through hostiles threatening on all sides.
Custer kept him in camp, where he died,

& was buried on the banks of the Big Goose
[where the city of Sheridan now stands]. In 1892,
his body was taken up & transferred to [Custer],
& laid to rest in the military burial ground there.

Sheridan on Custer
at the Battle of Yellow Tavern, 1864

Custer's charge was brilliantly executed.
Beginning at a walk, he increased this to a trot,
then, at full speed, rushed on the enemy. . . .

Time

Fireflies float over the night battlefield, eyemotes of the Great Mystery.
When is this, anyway, before or after?
Wherever they were born & raised, the soldiers found their ways to
here where Time
converges, meditation
within which that maker of light arranges & fuels the stars.

The Dead:

BLOOD & SAGE

March 17, 1876: The Ponies

A cavalry detachment attacked a Sioux village,
but had to withdraw through lingering winter,
ignominiously. Accurate Indians had shot
too many horses out from under them,

& they'd been forced for the first time
to abandon a comrade to certain torture,
but they'd captured several hundred ponies
whose throats they slashed during retreat

southward. Lieutenant Bourke recalled,
"It was pathetic to hear the dismal trumpeting
of the dying creatures as the breath of life
rushed through several windpipes at once."

Following in the hills, the Sioux heard their ponies
calling out to them while dying.
Even unto now, sleepless in their village, they tell
of the pitiful deaths of the ponies.

Custer on Poker

After General Sheridan communicated his resolve to me,
I proceeded directly to the lodge
where I found the two chiefs reclining lazily
upon their couches of buffalo robes. When I informed them

that if by sundown the following day their villages did
not come in to the protection of the fort,
both of them would be hanged
and troops sent to pursue their people, I could see

that both became instantly and unmistakably
interested in what I said,
but not a muscle of their warrior-like faces moved,
their eyes neither brightened nor quailed.

Luck

Breaking his vow,
Custer played a little "Hold-Em," but got gut-shot
twice in a row
by the river. The three-card flop, the turn,
the river—how
to play this goddamned bedevilin' game of intuition

& the laws of average
hovering in mirage. All these ifs & would-have-beens,
& how not
to fall in love with your hand? . . . Okay, he'd make his last
loose suicidal call until
the next one. If this were six-card stud, he'd

be way ahead,
but in an old poker adage he might or mightn't have heard,
patience is leverage. . . .
Benteen plays to & hits his running hearts! Again, the General
curses his luck
& flips his trips into the muck.

Saint Custer

Custer sensed a sequence of his selves,
saw himself in his mind's eye in photographs—
boy, cadet, officer, Indian fighter;
& what next?—in his heart's eye in paintings:

ditto. But if, as the saints seemed to say,
eternity is now, he'd always been *this* age,
here, hadn't he? Just shave, goddamnit,
he reminded himself, before you cut your nose off.

The Lightning

Prairie darkness except for the murmur of flowers until
the branched power struck. Then, blare of brightness, sear
of aura, a turning toward him of everything on earth,
the Strange One holding a white calf in his chest like breath.

Bourke: Shadow Memory

Many of Crook's infantry had never sat in a saddle,
none of these mules had ever been saddled,
but the cavalry officers ordered equestrian lessons,
and I never saw so much fun in my life.
For a mile in every direction the valley filled
with bucking mules, broken saddles, busted infantry,
and applauding spectators. The entire command
took a half holiday to witness these ludicrous mishaps.
When I recall such scenes, I laugh again as heartily
as on that bright June day in 1876.

Legend

What did it signify, then, that as the 1200 men
of the 7th Cavalry Regiment set out
in a two-mile column from Fort Abraham Lincoln
in mists of that early May morning,

they beheld a mirage: themselves in the sky,
there they were, wavery but clear where
some had before seen sylvan landscapes,
or lakes, or huge fish that once swam here? . . .

But now the soldiers themselves were caravan,
but bodiless, each man or horse or wagon in a kind
of trance. Even when Custer halted the column,
they all moved in apparitional undulation,

staying but going, undetermined, willful, in spelled
passage so beautiful, so biblical,
but more: as though they'd been here before,
as though they'd be here forever; but, no, as though

the column in all that vast language of sky
had only marked time, for them, for synchrony,
as though that legend awaiting them,
already written, could, as it were, continue.

Historical Ambiguity

As the 7th departed, Colonel Gibbon remarked,
"Now Custer, don't be greedy but wait for us."
Custer replied, "No, I will not."

Elizabeth Remembers the Regiment

There was a unity of movement about them
that made the column at a distance seem

like a broad dark ribbon
stretched smoothly over the plains.

Confluence

Custer's troop included a sixteen-piece band mounted
on white horses, but these could
not accompany him

past the confluence of the Powder & Yellowstone, except
for the horses. The musicians played goodbye
to the formidable 7th,

white horses rode off like notes of music soon
to be held in collective memory
by the Sioux & Cheyenne.

Loneliness: Letter to Elizabeth, June 17, 1876

We rode through the remains of an Indian village.
I was at the head of the column,
and suddenly came upon a human skull
lying within an extinct fire. Nearby,

I found the uniform of a soldier.
The buttons on the overcoat held a "C,"
and the dress-coat had the yellow cord
of the cavalry uniform running through it. . . .

Some poor trooper had been a prisoner
in the hands of the savages. He was doubtless
tortured to death, probably burned.
The worst thought is that he died alone.

Bourke: Rosebud Moon Taunt Lure

Crazy Horse, rallying on the second line of heights,
became bold and impudent again.
His men rode up and down rapidly, sometimes

wheeling in circles, slapping
an indelicate portion of their persons at us,
beckoning us to come on.

Bourke: Rosebud Battle Scene

I passed one Crow Indian sitting on the ground,
not acting one bit hurt, watching the fight
between his people and the Sioux.
Sometimes, he'd yell like a madman.

Unable to stand, having been shot in the knee,
the bone shattered, his horse dead by his side,
he seemed so interested in the fight
as to forget his fatal wound.

After Rosebud: The Staring

One chief, probably Crazy Horse,
directed their movements
by signals made with a pocket mirror
or some other reflector. . . .

Persistent whooping, but
"the Indian voice
is less hoarse than the Caucasian,"
wrote correspondent John F. Finerty,

"and has a sort of wolfish bark to it,
doubtless the result of heredity,
because the Indians, for untold ages,
have been imitators of the vocal characteristics

of the prairie wolf. . . ." In any case,
eight days afterward,
about eighteen miles further westward,
in the neighboring valley of the Little Big Horn,

these same Sioux would again appear
at Custer's nightmare. In between,
Crazy Horse mirrored himself to ascertain
if he was the chosen one.

Coils

A holy man described his grandfather's journey
far to the south of the west. Curly listened, & remembered:
in that country, above a canyon, the warrior found the east-facing entrance

to a cave of white stone. Below him,
only the desert of lizards, of cactus & yucca, but risen
to surface in the cave, broken pots, shells, flint spear points, then

a rotted bag, a chert scraper, seeds,
& the ancient head of a turtle with turquoise eyes, then
an inverted basket coiled over a child's skull circled in necklaces

of pink beads: the child,
a girl, woke in his mind until he slept
to dream his coiled vision of the makers of baskets. . . .

Crazy Horse often filtered this story.
His own people were not buried, but no matter:
scaffolds are caves in air, &, in time, layers of wind cover the dead.

Many of his own loved ones
had joined that daughter speaking in his chest,
& the Great Everywhere Spirit shone in the turquoise eyes of that turtle.

Preamble: The Rifle

A few mornings after the battle along the Rosebud
which took place on what whites call June 17, 1876,
Crazy Horse took several boys back with him
to pick up scattered ammunition, shell cases,
lead from bullets spent against rocks,
arrow points, iron shoes from dead horses.
One boy found a rifle, its barrel in the mouth
of a suicide. He took rifle & scalp, but retched.
Crazy Horse told him to throw away the scalp:

The old way of fighting for coups is past.
These soldiers are not here with their women.
They are here to kill us, day and night,
during all the moons. That life is past
of fighting Crows and Snakes between hunts.
We have no time to dance. We must kill
as the soldiers kill, or we the people
will not be able to place our feet
upon the ground, anywhere, in our own land.

The Calls: Elizabeth to George
from Fort Lincoln, May 1876

Carter has returned and is chief trumpeter.
He really sounds the calls beautifully,
but his long-drawn notes make me heartsick,
for I do not wish to be reminded of the cavalry.

The Writing Life: Elizabeth to George
from Fort Lincoln, June 1876

I have this month's *Galaxy* with the Yellowstone article.
How fortunate you had left it with Mr. Sheldon.
You improve every time you write.

I am anxious about the one you sent by the Fort Buford mail.
The mail was dropped in the Yellowstone.
They must have tried to dry it

before the fire, for all our letters are scorched. . . .

I think to ride as you do and write is wonderful. Nothing
daunts you in your wish to improve. I wish
your lines had fallen among

literary people, but wouldn't have you anything but a soldier.

The wildflowers here are a revelation, almost the first
sweet-scented I have ever known.
The house hosts bouquets,

and I walk from room to room in . . . vertigo, trying not
to think of you. Do you not see
your life is precious? . . .

I shall go to bed now and dream of you in flowers.

Romance

The above letter was never received by Custer who, by then,
lived beyond the reach of letters.
It was returned to Elizabeth unopened. For decades,
she kept it unopened.

O how the romance of this can charge the breast: Elizabeth
survived him fifty-seven years,
never remarried, was buried beside a few
bones at the Point

where the twain twine into sunsets above the river
as the 7th Cavalry appears again
in the serrated clouds, & early summer thunder
beats like a broken heart.

Stepping in Footsteps: Lieutenant Godfrey's Account

June 24th we passed a great many camping-places,
all appearing to be of nearly the same strength.
One would naturally suppose these were the successive
camping-places of the same village, when, in fact,
they were the continuous camps of the several bands.

Voice

Two days before the battle, Sitting Bull
keeps his penance: at the Sun Dance ceremony,
fifty bits of skin are cut from each arm;
next, a daylong staring at the sun until,

in his vision, enemy Indians & white soldiers
fall head-down into his campfires
like grasshoppers, & a voice cries,
I give you these because they have no ears.

Unknown to Him

Custer realized that while with an excellent field glass he
could scarcely see that the distant speck was a horseman,
the Indian by his side knew what the horseman signalled.
They have eyes like hawks, the General muttered, while,
as if in answer & entirely unknown to him, a hawk
positioned the General's head in its telepathic sight.

Mind's Eye

After scout Red Star handed the message to Custer
that the Sioux camp had been sighted,
he knocked over his coffee cup—
dark blood in the dirt.

Directions

Yesterday, Sitting Bull, not far away,
offered buckskin bags of tobacco & willow bark
to the sacred directions, & prayed that his people be saved,
& heard that he'd been heard.

Today, Half Yellow Face, Crow scout,
offers tobacco to the four winds. Curious,
Custer strides over to ask why. "Because," says the scout,
"you and I are going home."

Nearer to Thee

(Fort Lincoln, June 25, 1876)

After the noon meal, an informal service,
for this was Sunday.
For this was Sunday, & the women pined
for their husbands,
for their husbands hunting Sioux & Cheyenne.
In the gathering fore-
boding of the afternoon, the women sang:

Tho like a wanderer,
The sun gone down,
Darkness be over me,
My rest a stone.
Yet in my dream I'd be
Nearer, my God, to Thee,
Nearer, my God, to Thee,
Nearer to Thee! . . .

After the noon meal, an informal service,

    Tho like a wanderer,

for this was Sunday.

    The sun gone down,

For this was Sunday, & the women pined

    Darkness be over me,

for their husbands,

    My rest a stone.

for their husbands hunting Sioux & Cheyenne.

    Yet in my dream I'd be

In the gathering fore-

Nearer, my God, to Thee,

boding of the afternoon, the women sang:

Nearer, my God, to Thee,
Nearer to Thee. . . .

The Hill: A Crow Scout's Story

Then we found the Sioux trails coming together.
Then Custer told me to go and save my life.
My ammunition low, I made a circle around.
I found a dead Sioux. I took his ammunition,

and got out, but stayed near until the fight.
I rode to a high butte east of the battlefield
where I could see. From that high place,
I saw that Custer was the last man to stand.

The Curse

The boy Dives Backward
was catching grasshoppers for fish bait.
In cupped hands,
he'd carry them down the bank to his uncle.
This time, as he started his descent,

he heard what sounded like thousands of horses, & saw
enemy Indians ride by,
& bluecoats following in their dust.
The soldiers drove on toward the boy's camp. The boy released
a plague from his hands.

Deconstruction

It was too hot, & the bluecoats
were not wearing their blue coats.

Karma

The first soldier to die was Sergeant Heyn
of G Company, shot through the chest.

Dust

Crazy Horse was first to cross the river
toward Custer & his bluecoats.
"Then," recalled Short Buffalo,
"there was too much dust—
I could not see any more."

Cheyenne Chief Two Moons saw
that the dead soldiers were coated
with white dust. On the plains:
skeletons of the brontosaurus
& its co-inhabiters,

& then this dust at the site
of the battle of the Little Bighorn—
& the fact that when we breathe
we breathe subatomic particles
once breathed by Crazy Horse & Custer.

Crazy Horse in Stillness

As Crazy Horse in stillness rides toward Custer,
more & more warriors magnetize behind him
who is the point of an arrow hovering
at the edge of a cloud of dust in the brain
where it oscillates, shudders, & stays.

Red

Curly's father instructed him
to cut open a snapping turtle
& eat its still-beating heart.
Thirty years later, in battle,
a red sky snapped in him.

Medicine

A tiny man of deerskin,
buffalo wool his hair,
tied to Soldier Wolf's
left breast. In battle,

the little rawhide man
becomes the warrior,
Soldier Wolf invisible
who cannot be killed

unless the bullet
strikes this homunculus,
buffalo wool his hair,
which it won't.

Presence

Chief Gall saw the Great Spirit
riding a black pony,
overlooking all in that heat & blood,
perfectly happy.

The Bear

One foreclaw hooked
the soldier's right shoulder blade
& tore it out entirely.
The other foreclaw
tore all the flesh

from the right side.
One hindclaw tore open
the lower abdomen,
letting out the bowels & badly
scarifying the left leg,

while the other hindclaw
tore muscles from the right thigh
from groin to knee—
during this transformation
of warrior into grizzly.

Crying News

A Cheyenne warrior east of his camp along the river
held up a blue shirt with the 7th Cavalry insignia

on its collar—this he'd seen on the shoulders of soldiers
who had killed his mother on the Washita.

"This day," he shouted, tears running with paint,
"my heart is again made glad." Waving the shirt,

he rode through one camp after another to his own,
crying news of his heart made glad again.

The Thrill of White History

In Chief Two Moons' narration, a story thrills
within this sentence: "I found two or three soldiers killed
and saw one running away to reach the high hills beyond,
and we took after him, and killed him."

How did this soldier happen to be here at all, so far west
on the Little Bighorn? How old is he? What is he thinking
as he runs from his overwhelmed comrades? Does he pray,
or remember his mother, or curse Custer?

Does he think he has a chance? Does he think to shoot himself
before savages do what they will do to him? As we whites
hear Two Moons, we imagine being this soldier, running through
our self-made nightmare to reach the hills.

Furnace

By the time Custer reached, if he did,
the hill on which he might have died,
he would have realized his command
was doomed. Half his men were down,

the rest forced into groups hemmed in
by Sioux & Cheyenne on horses & afoot.
From the moment the 7th froze in its
final position, they had a snowball's.

Geometry

When Custer could not cross the Little Big Horn,
he fought directly east for the high bluffs,
behind which hundreds of Indians hid
who rose to meet him as his men advanced.

Custer, surprised, attempted to charge through
to the northeast, but met such withering fire
as to be forced to lower ground, by which time
the enemy had crossed the river & filled

all draws to the north, thus compelling Custer
to fight & feel his way west & south,
which accounts for the finding of the bodies
lying in quite a perfect circle.

The Paper It's Written On

At the millisecond of death, he is still on his horse.
A bullet has severed his brain-stem, & he is dead,
but in this instant even he does not know this.
The last strobe of consciousness is passing out of him.
Dead in the saddle, his dead body still on auto
before he disassembles, his horse unaware of his limbo,
he is the treaty imposed & signed with smoke & x's.

After-Image

During the time between his technical death
& his fall from his horse, Custer saw a river—
this one lit bluegold from within—

across which Elizabeth was walking a pony,
but motionlessly, on moveless color & water.
Once his dead body had gone under,

she looked back over her shoulder.
He could see her, but she, stricken
in grief, seemed blind, & moved on.

Calf Amber

Something to show you, Libbie said to Custer,
& opened her mouth wide. Her teeth
were gems, two perfect rows—ruby,
diamond, amethyst, emerald, their colors
dream-flawless—but before he could kiss her,
she was meadow, through which buffalo grazed,

one calf's pupil holding both of them as though
in amber. Where did time go? he wondered
from wherever he was; where
does time go? she wondered also.
It's fortunate you & I still know how not
to classify these two, lovers in amber.

Fusion

Sioux shaman Black Elk,
thirteen at the time of the battle,
afterward walked among the dead soldiers,
"not sorry at all . . . happy,"
though the smells of gore sickened him.

He surely noticed, on heads where scalps
had been peeled off,
again & again the same map
of what this country would become,
the blacker seepage as reservations

predicted in these remains,
& how the red darkened in insect summer,
& how dust hovered & shone,
&, as night reclaimed the hills,
their own uranium of grievous joy.

Cash

At first they seemed leaves,
uppersides of the cottonwood,
the talking tree,
but were greenbacks
whispering white presidents
through the grass
among the dead who were paid
prior to their translation
into language where
you can't buy anything
from the sutler
because there is no paper,
or metal, or stone, or goods
you can weigh, or measure,
so all that stuff
might as well litter
the storied slopes
like leaves from albums
green with promise
of good food, of whiskey,
of dance which requires
a body

onto which you pulled
your boots that now have
no feet to go to
but Sioux.

The Charm

The boy Black Elk found something gold
in a soldier's pocket, round & gold,

attached to a long gold chain.
It made the sound of a ticking beetle,

so he wore it, amulet, around his neck.
That night, the beetle slept, but

Black Elk learned to encourage
its arrow feet to circle again.

Awls

Good Fox told this story he was told:
two Cheyenne women reached Custer's body,

& said to him, "You smoked the pipe with us,
our chiefs told you you'd be killed

if you made war on us again. You would
not listen. Now you will hear better."

From beaded cases they took awls
& worked them deep into Custer's ears.

Teeth

When George, who was called "Autie," was four,
he had to have a tooth drawn.
His father told him, "Be a good soldier."
When they got to the doctor, Autie took his seat,
& the pulling began. The forceps slipped off, were

reconfigured for a second try. The doctor,
after much perspiration, succeeded. Autie
never even scrunched. On the battlefield,
a Cheyenne woman chopped out a molar
for a souvenir. Autie never even scrunched.

The Tooth

After the beheading, they found
the one gold tooth in Custer's mouth.
They propped open his jaws,

cut away his upper lip,
& looked into the tooth in firelight.
It was like a small television

tuned to the news, & a white man
in a white suit was already
stepping down onto the moon.

Dixon: The Altar

"The hollow silence of these hill slopes,
the imperishable valour
of two-hundred and seventy-seven men
who laid their lives on a blood-red altar,

until the one lone figure of the great leader
lifted his unavailing sword
against a howling horde of savage warriors—
glittering for a moment in the June sunlight,

then falling to the earth baptized
with blood—
is the solemn picture forever to hang
in the nation's gallery of battles."

Wakan Tanka

For a time   after the battle   dust assumed
the form   of a white buffalo   grazing the dead.

Necessities

   Next day, toward sunset,
                the Indians fired the grass in the valley,
& Reno's men,
        through rifts of smoke,
              watched them move, slowly,
   upriver toward the Bighorns
          where it would be time, again,
to cut new lodge-poles
       & begin fattening their thin ponies.

The Token

More than twenty Sioux dead
were laid out on scaffolds erected
in one burial lodge, their faces painted

in ceremonial colors, brightly shaped.
When Crazy Horse visited,
he was the only one there who needed

to breathe, but he was not alone, & asked
his friends to prepare his place, & wept,
& left his heart behind him when he left.

Blood & Sage

For days, the smell of rotting blood
mixes with sage
& wafts over the landscape.

Mice smell it, & coyotes,
& snakes with their tongues,
& even, in their own ways, grasses,

& even, in their own ways, rocks,
& even, in their own ways, the dead.
Some of the living smell it while awake,

some while sleeping. The dead smell it
day & night, & are restless, Custer
among them. Crazy Horse smells it

while he hunts during a dream: the buffalo
smell it, & retreat in front of him,
sickened: he abandons the hunt,

but a hot wind blows the blood & sage
into his village until
his people understand, & move on.

Three Days Later

From a distance, dark hillside splotches seemed buffalo skins,
other pale objects seemed dead buffalo,

but these were dead horses & dead naked soldiers, bloated
in summer insect heat.

Under each porcupine cluster of arrows, in grass-sticky blood,
another dead trooper, usually beheaded. . . .

Words of Goes-Ahead
Translated & Transcribed by Dr. Dixon

When I heard that Custer had been killed I said,
"He is a man to fight the enemy. He loved to fight,
but if he fights and is killed, he will have to be killed."

Revelations

A strange looking object directly in our path,
& more than a mile distant. Too large to be human,
yet in color & appearance it resembled no animal.
We reached it, a white horse, dead & bloated
almost to bursting in the day's white heat.
At Fort Sedgwick, some time before, we'd seen
one company of cavalry mounted on white horses,
& this, no doubt, was one of these, no doubt.
With this sabre, we puncture its carcass to spew
putrescence of truth into our arrogant faces.

Souls: Captain Gibson of Benteen's Battalion

Eight o'clock on the morning of the twenty-seventh
we saw clouds of dust arising five miles in front—
Terry with Gibbon's command. This explained
the Indians' sudden departure.

Can you imagine our relief and gratitude when
we saw those troops coming to succor us, taking us
right out of the jaws of death, and such
a horrible death?

Of course, we inquired for Custer and his men,
but to our utter surprise and uneasiness learned
that Terry and Gibbon had seen nor heard
nothing of them. Then,

H Company ventured out for further information.
At Custer's battle ground, we gained positive knowledge:
two hundred and fifty souls, every last
man of them killed. . . .

On the twenty-eighth the command moved to the site,
and interred the dead. My men buried the General and Tom
and their young schoolboy brother. I had them placed beside
each other, their graves marked. . . .

I have lived in a great many places, slept in many beds,
but that one grass hill where we buried the brothers Custer
and hundreds of others is the one to which, every night
before I sleep, I return. . . .

On the Evening of the 29th

We bathed in the river
& climbed again to where
Custer's men had fallen.

Moonlit vultures did
not bother to lift such
sated bodies into flight,
coyotes stood still until
we clapped, & that
other animal filled the air,
drawing our vomit
into our throats, but
this time we could
swallow it. We,
no ones ourselves,
knew we were history,
this finest evening
of our lives, this odor
of our luck, our fame.

Tidings

I cup my hands over my mouth & halloo Custer
in the world of the dead: *Long Hair,*
your one terrible anxiety, that which you so feared,
& which kept you awake at night—
you didn't have to worry: the Indians didn't escape.

Elizabeth: The Legend of Rain-in-the-Face

Iron Horse had come to smoke the pipe and ask
that the Father in Washington spare the life
of his brother, Rain-in-the-Face, who had slain
two unarmed whites, first shooting them, then
with his stone mallet beating out their breaths,
then filling the bodies with arrows.
                              Months later,
Rain escaped and joined the Sitting Bull hostiles.
At Little Big Horn, this fiend incarnate

concentrated his hate and cut out the heart
of that gallant, loyal, and lovable man
who had once captured him, our brother Tom.

A.D., First Light

Libbie lay half asleep listening to rain
against window or canvas where was she,
& when? Autie would kiss her awake,
or never again? Sleep, then, she told herself,
& could almost stay, but couldn't. Rain
carried first light along in its wings,
& he lay dead with the light, archangel.

Place

A year later, a scouting expedition camped on the site
of the abandoned Sioux village. Wolves kept them
half-awake, & then someone felt something
on his face, & yelled "Snakes." It was a lizard,

almost a foot long, greenblack in firelight,
& hundreds more, aswarm around them.
The men hacked with sabres, then tried
to get some zees, but the lizards returned.

Verdi

When, where we once thought he was, we dug for Custer,
we found the remains of an old squaw, desiccated,
recognizable. How she happened there
under the General's marker

was anybody's guess, as was where he was now.
Her face-skin had retreated to her cheek-
bones, exposing her ivories,
which were playing.

How could she have known that European aria?
Someone spread a flag over her visage,
but once you'd seen her, you
could never not hear her,

so we searched for evidential broken earth where Custer
must have turned over in his grave, but
couldn't find him, & the squaw
keeps playing underground.

Rout Route

In time, every whatnot—canteens, brass buttons, spoons—
& several harmonicas uncovered
by metal detectors.

Clef

Ten or twelve thousand years ago megafauna—
mammoth, mastodon, ground sloth, giant beaver,
saber-toothed tiger, short-faced bear & the rest—

died out, but some bones are not yet dust,
thus this ravine into which a dying bluecoat
plunged his head, something, if we could hear,

in his facial bones vibing the remains
of another eon, & vice versa, bones
singing to bones in melodies of extinction.

Memoir: Pretty Voice Eagle, 1909

I was not there at the Little Big Horn
but saw General Custer before he left Fort Lincoln.

We asked him not to fight the Sioux but
go to them as friend. He promised and

we asked him to raise his hand to God not
to fight the Sioux, and he raised his hand.

He asked us to go west to tell those roaming Sioux
return to the reservation for horses, clothing,

food. After he talked, we left, but soon heard
he and his men were killed. If he'd given us time

when he raised his hand to God not to fight the Sioux,
we would have gone ahead, he would have lived. . . .

If the whites can kill that fatal disease, consumption,
I'll be grateful. . . . I think often and often

of our camps in buffalo time, the meat and the hides—
my need for them seems like a disease.

Custer from His Grave

Twenty years after I was killed,
I heard my wife's book.
Only one sentence reminds me of this place
where I am now, among others,
diffused but definite,

everything going still as I died
with this genre of future in my mind.
Elizabeth had been walking with one of my officers
under cottonwoods along a river,
Dakota Territory: "Without the least warning,

in the dead stillness of that desolate spot,
we suddenly came upon
a group of young Indian warriors
seated in their motionless way in the underbrush."
As they are with me here.

The Waking

Midwinter thaw—
insects above the snow, the frail
long-legged fliers.

Interlude

Now, sweet-grass & cherry bark
in the coals, the fragrance
of well being.

Annuities

A pony wearing a white man's
tophat, two holes cut out
for its ears.

$

Silver dollars hammered into disks
for the warriors' hair—
autumn.

Wife

Black Shawl beads
a pair of moccasins with lightning streaks,
his vision.

Eclipse

The men run out
& shoot arrows at the animal
eating the moon.

Sapwood:

WINGDUST

Cockroach Rainbow

In the cabin of the whites, these
ran from scraps of fat set out
for a dog. Crazy Horse's skin seemed
to crawl with these pale crawlers. . . .

He crushed some with a stick:
their shells/wings/softparts glistened,
as though color itself blessed
him for its release.

Jack-in-the-Box

In another settler's cabin,
Crazy Horse turned a metal crank
on a wooden box. Something
flew up into his face, then

jerked & bounced—a head
painted with stars & stripes.
He thought to restore the demon,
later to trick the children,

but brought down his rifle butt.
The thing seemed to spring at him,
& jeer him, before he bashed it
into a satisfying facelessness.

Raisins

He returned to his village with two sacks of raisins from the dead.
He called the children, held one sack open, then the other.
As the children laughed & filled their hands & cheeks,

he tasted in his mind the sweet berries of the whites,
but knew that . . . But be here *now*, he reminded himself:
in the happiness of children eating sun-dried berries, there is *now*.

Rocking Chair

In another cabin, Crazy Horse sat in a chair set
on curved runners, pushed his feet against
the floor, & rocked, this movement resting him

after what he'd done. He kept rocking, leaned
his head back, closed his eyes, & almost slept,
except for the dead, so close, & now drawing

flies. . . . The heat of hate, & then this, this
calming, so curious, & these people westering
with their guns & furniture. He rocked

into evening, the last light buzzing reddish & diffuse
from so far away it could have been a voice
lost in a last story somewhere, years before.

The Herd

Once in the later years when buffalo were few,
in the years when Crazy Horse often
rode out across the land alone,
Oglala scouts found a small herd, & there,

downwind on a knoll near the grazing animals,
saw their Strange One resting, gun across his knees.
They watched him for a long time, believing
he'd dreamt the herd into being.

Mother

Crazy Horse saw a woman so enormous in belly
she seemed to carry all the Lakota,
all the world.

He liked thinking of this: rivers from source to egress, hills
ever blossoming forth, herds swelling in her
until their birth.

Crazy Horse Laughs

In 1877 his friend He Dog decided to move to where the whites ordered.
He stood in council—Crazy Horse did not attend—& said,
"All who love their wife and children,

let them come with me. All who want these killed, let them stay."
Afterwards, in Crazy Horse's lodge, He Dog heard
that two whites had visited

with gifts: cigars & a knife. Therefore, of course, they could not be trusted.
"Does this mean," He Dog asked, "you will be my enemy
if I move across the creek?" . . .

Crazy Horse laughed, said He Dog, "laughed in my face, & said,
'I am no white man! They are the ones that make rules
for other people, that say,

*If you stay here, it is peace, but move to the other side of this line
and I will kill you all.* I don't hold with deadlines.
Camp where you please.'"

The Resolution

Crazy Horse considered traveling to Washington.
Practiced eating with a white man's fork.
Asked where, in that iron horse, he could sleep,
or relieve himself. Hearing of structures

with people living overhead, he imagined
strata of spirits walking above his lodge.
Asked his yellow pinto, who danced assent,
but Washington was a bayonet, twice withdrawn.

Captain Bourke Describes Crazy Horse in 1877

A man who looked quite young,
not over thirty years old,
five feet eight inches high,
lithe and sinewy, a scar in the face,
expression one of quiet dignity,

but morose, dogged, tenacious, and melancholy.
He behaved with stolidity,
like a man who realized he must give in to Fate,
but would do so as sullenly as possible.
While talking to Frank Grouard, his countenance

lit up with genuine pleasure,
but to all others he was, at least in the final days
of his coming upon the reservation,
gloomy and reserved. I never heard an Indian
mention his name save in terms of respect.

Resignation in Autumn Rain

First a few drops,
then splatters,
& soon the whole rock
on which he squats has darkened.
He rubs fingers

over its wet surface, & feels grit. Rock
is soft in time,
life is dust & pumice,
late moons shrivel grass & scatter leaves
along the river,

vultures themselves feed worms,
& soon snow
will blanket the scaffolds.
The Great Mystery takes everything back,
even rock.

Coming In

Before he led his people in,
Crazy Horse remembered the tight band
of green hide wrapped
around the base of the scrotum

to dry & cut off circulation, thus
removing the snarl
from even the most aggressive male until
he'd pull a travois. . . .

Report to the Commissioner of Indian Affairs

When I arrived at this agency,
I found Crazy Horse and his band,
consisting of about 1,100 people,
encamped two miles north.

Crazy Horse manifests a sullen,
morose disposition; evidently
a man of small capacity,
he has been brought into notoriety

by his stubborn will and brute courage.
His dictatorial manners, and disregard
for the comfort of his people, have caused
dissatisfaction among them,

and his want of truthfulness
with the military
has rendered him unpopular
with the leading men of his band,

who have drawn off from him
and say they are determined
to carry out their promises
to obey orders and keep the peace.

All the other Sioux chiefs are doing well,
and it seems hardly possible
that they will ever
take up arms again. . . .

(James Irwin, Indian Agent
Red Cloud Agency, Nebraska
August 25, 1877)

Annuity Supplies, 1877

As yet we have not had time or opportunity to make examination
of the annuity supplies received by us, but as soon
as we get into our new buildings we will make examination
of them and submit a special report in relation thereof. . . .

Patent Office

Crazy Horse faxed a query to D.C.
Like hell he did. Or if he did, Prez
Bureaucracy wasn't answering.
When will I have my promised agency?
His question turned brown in spilled ersatz
sponged up with a dried tongue.

The Leatherstocking Tales

Just before his fatal wounding,
as Crazy Horse passed a room at Fort Robinson,
he saw, through an open door, a shelf of books.

He'd known books, but never so many, in such order.
He knew these objects were covered in leather,
but these were shiny, with gold signs on their backs,

& flashed in his mind a night he'd ridden off alone
& killed two whites in their cabin,
& thrown their one book into their fire:

it did not flame, it smoldered,
the fire could not penetrate
the thin layers of black meanings:

he became afraid, this fear deepening in him
as he neared his village, this fear
never again left him, never: whites stared

into these objects as he stared into pondwater
or the night sky which sometimes shot arrows afire:
the bayonet struck: there were as many books

in the approaching wagons of the whites as his people
still had breaths to breathe—it struck again—& these could
not be understood, befriended, or burned.

Seeing & Knowing: Grouard's Testimony

I did not see the death thrust
as it was given
from behind the captive,
or know whether
it was dealt by the sentinel,
with his bayonet,
or by an officer
with his sword.
The next instant
I saw Crazy Horse
turn completely around
on his left foot,
and fall over,
backwards. I knew
he had been stabbed,
but could not see
who did it.

Government Protection

After the promised protection at Fort Robinson,
Doctor McGillicuddy, friendly spirit, said,
"I wedged my way in between the guard
and found Crazy Horse on his back,

grinding his teeth and frothing at the mouth,
blood trickling from a bayonet wound above the hip,
and the pulse weak and missing beats,
and I saw that he was done for.". . .

At five o'clock that afternoon,
the doctor administered a shot of morphine.
A kerosene lamp smoked beside them. . . .
When the first dose of morphine wore down,

the Indian received another, & now the buffalo
wash themselves in moaning wallows on the plains,
& all the women he has known
fly above him in their blankets, holding

suckling children, & air is arrow,
arrow everywhere, the moon dimming & bursting,
& *thwack*, the flag, unlike an eagle's wing above the fort,
thwacks in wind, each time like an enlightenment.

Duration

Sources believe
that Crazy Horse
was stabbed twice

by a scared private
whose first name
was William, but,

in any case,
stabbed twice. The killer
thrust his bayonet

into the captive's side, with-
drew it, took aim
& plunged it into

Crazy Horse again,
this time deep
into his kidneys. . . .

In the space between
the two strikes
the victim tried

to twist loose
from constraining arms but
couldn't but

he'd by then with-
drawn except
from pain except

from regret but
who could have known
the motion would slow

to this slow?—
the thrust, then
duration during which

he realized again
the actions of his life
when he threw a berry

at Black Buffalo Woman
when they were children
when he killed his first

enemy the Omaha woman
whose bloodthick hair & scalp
sickened him when

his people elected him
the holy shirt when
it was taken back when

the herds beat
in his chest during
the night's hunt, & more,

& countless more, then
the second piercing
of the government blade, then

the long slow undesired
agonized falling
into legend.

The Passive

Crazy Horse was bayoneted at Fort Robinson
in early September, 1877. For several hours
he lay on the floor, unconscious, then
woke up, then spoke what for him were many words,
variously remembered, then died.

He was wrapped in a red blanket
& was placed on a platform on a hill.
His father & mother mourned beside him
day & dark, & kept pigs & wolves
from his flesh. To assist them,

a fence was put up around him,
& women packed lodges onto travois in the sky,
& the great Oglala dead appeared to welcome & guide him
home. & the years after were counted in suffering,
& nobody was responsible for anything.

Drying Grass Moon, 1877

Crazy Horse placed on a scaffold.
He no longer had to speak, or breathe.

He no longer had to drink, or eat.
He no longer had to sleep, or wake.

His parents left with his heart,
moving closer to him with every distance—

another way into the world of visions,
other ways into the world of visions.

The Trail

Mourners drifted the camp in white blankets.
The trail to their beloved Strange One began
up there in the white afterland among animals
whose legs were stars, among warriors
whose arrows & axes were stars. The mourners
mourned, but night returned with stories
that glimpsed the dangerous trail for which,
all his faithful life, the dead one had prepared.

"Anticipatory Breach"

It's when you have a series of contracts,
& the other party, whyever, breaks the first, &/or
another, or others, & this breach of contract

forces you to say, *no more*. Crazy Horse studied
lawbooks, & the people's razed villages,
& the attitudes of the scaffolded dead & said,

no more, & when he died, paper shrouds
drifted over the sacred land from Washington
as though he were a mummy, & could be wrapped.

Companions

After Crazy Horse was murdered,
his favorite pony, a pinto,
was gashed in the sides & legs.
Loved ones who saw the blood
answered in kind on their own bodies,
& sounds of grief flew up
into the pony's ears all night
from circles of mourners around it.
The pinto wondered whether
its master were near
& would ride him far away
from the keening & weeping—
at least it smelled such images
in its mind for the rest of its life,
& grew relentlessly lonely
for the rider & that journey.

Wingdust

At Fort Robinson Crazy Horse dies in an adjutant's office
with windows in it, & a cast iron stove. The walls
right-angle into one another, & the wide-board floor.
He seems to hear a moth fluttering in a web,

but cannot find it, though his eyes are closed.
Moth wingdust stirs the hair in his nostrils.
In the haze of McGillicuddy's morphine,
we commune with him now in this fusion of dream & time.

L.A. Freeway

As they were fighting for the knife,
Crazy Horse, by accident, cut his own wrists.
His blood seeped into his buckskin shirt
& into dirt. His blood dried. His blood flew away
to here, & we breathe it. . . .

In our lungs, buffalo herd in Crazy Horse's blood.
They reach a river, its fringe of cottonwoods
& willows. When we close our eyes,
we appear under trees as the buffalo enter.
We breathe deeply, once, thrice, a few more times

& the blood sparkles into night stars
in remote blackness, into history, the plains
stretching away forever. Crazy Horse's blood
is as old as the stars in us from which we are made,
in which, in traffic, we almost remember everything.

Scenarios

Custer sought out Crazy Horse.
The two sat under a willow near a river,
facing one another. I wanted to tell you,
said Custer: like all the rest, my employer
is down-sizing. They've offered me a buy-out,
I've agreed to take it, this is the right time,
Libbie and I will settle in the Capital,
there's a chance I'll become
the Great Father, and if
I do, I'll send
for you.

The tree lost its leaves twice,
thrice. Crazy Horse didn't want to ask,
& didn't. If Long Hair said anything more,
Tasunke Witko didn't hear, but stared
into the white's forehead until, in the brainfolds,
he saw cobblestones & people, whole cities
of stone buildings, & white people. One
lifted his tall black hat. An eagle
flew out, & hovered. In one
of its eyes, the herds receded,
one calf bawling

at the rear.

During the Moon of Snow Blindness in What Is Called the Year 1905, Crazy Horse Visits the Steamship Nebraska

One of the last places for him on earth,
this ark.

This night, at mid-Atlantic, he appears
in the ship's hold, in the pen where

the two buffalo of Cody's Wild West Show,
their legs atremble, sleep while dreaming
of swimming commensurate plains in a sea
of their own kind.

Crazy Horse passes through
planks & animal flesh, startles the half-dozen
long-horned steers.

In the Indian-packed stern,
only Red Fox, his beloved nephew, almost wakens
to his aura.

The ship plunges toward Liverpool,
a motley of props packed in its hold, a whole
stagecoach whose white passengers for four years
would surrender their scalps across Europe.
Crazy Horse,

conflicted spirit, finds the chest
in which is folded a dyed shirt
on which is sewn a strip of beadwork descended
from his mothers.

Now, he becomes a dragonfly—
it's the only way—& absorbs a bead for each facet
of his wraparound eyes,

& flies toward us
across the night waves with at least this.

Custer in Cyberspace

Liquid crystal displays in his helmet,
a double click for "Garryowen,"
Custer charges in, again, the 7th's guidon
vivid above him, Libbie at his side,

& why not? & why not the Indians' throats
in his dogs' jaws? & why not
a cool day, his men rested, & each death
in slow motion mixed in with three clicks

of wildflower perfume mixed in with her,
here, where no one can see them
on their blanket on this hill as he comes
into paradisal revision of the Little Big Horn?

Welcome

Crazy Horse called Custer over
to see something growing horizontally
from the trunk of a riverbank black willow.
At first, Custer saw nothing extraordinary,
but there from shadow reached a wrist
with its perfect hand on which a ring—
silver, incised with symbols—glittered
from its middle finger. The palm-up hand
seemed welcoming, submissive, as though
to draw the viewer into where its body
fused with wood. When, with two hands,
Custer gripped it to remove the ring,
Crazy Horse grimaced, knowing
the willow would never let go.

Timewarp

Crazy Horse sees spotlights in the sky—
a new shopping center, stores
for sneakers, liquor, & lingerie along its mall,
one book emporium discounting remainders
on the glory of the Sioux, & Custer.

The spotlights crisscross like tipi poles.
He will visit that place,
but not today. Today, herds still migrate
beyond the shafts of acetylene light,
so he urges his horse forward,

his people following, their travois
streaks of afterimage in sky prairie.
Again, for a split moment, he understands nothing
forward or back to the beginning, but then
regains his essence, & rides on.

Custer Daydreaming

Custer looked into his rearview mirror:
the future gaining on him, buffalo galloping backwards
toward the sunset horizon, dustbowls eddying into being—silt swirls

in a frogpond when he was a boy.
He pressed the pedal & sped ahead, but the mirror
& its predictions could not be left behind: he felt stupid, & needed

gas. So what if he had to fill his tank
with roses & pterodactyls? Would the world outlast
the civilized & the savage, if only one cactus or speck of algae remained

to rebegin again?
Yes, the fucking traffic is worse
this time of day, this time tomorrow. Get a horse.

Luggage

At the airport, a gate change, Crazy Horse hustling
from one concourse to another. The moving walkway

ain't fast enough—he runs beside it like a dog
pulling a travois, he thinks. Just time
to split into the men's room for a piss, then
off on the double again. Boston or Cheyenne,
no matter. A cart beeps behind him,
its passengers leaning on canes, decrepit. Suddenly,
his breast fills with the pure water of being, of joy.

Lice

Custer & Crazy Horse listened to both sides
of the abortion question. Each in his own way
looked over canyons behind his own eyes
& saw raptors whose gaze focused on mice

in whose fur those tiny logicians lived.
Summer grasses burned like technicolor foetuses
marked "Exhibit A," arguments droned on,
eagles & hawks flew into primal thermals

into time before beings were born. The lice,
who had provoked that whole damnable business,
plied their trade, clawed trails, sucked blood.
The two men kept their minds on the lice.

Eyes Glazing Over

Crazy Horse, Custer, & the white buffalo sat down to talk,
but the buffalo said nothing. Crazy Horse also
said nothing, as, in good faith, Custer rambled on,
his head filled with churches whose steeples
impaled the Indians & the herds. Custer did

not know this, but would it have mattered if he had?
At some time during the cavalryman's peroration,
the white buffalo decided she'd be a constellation,
her belly filled with light years & stars over the plains,
where bored & wily Crazy Horse was already waiting.

1950: The Head

Crazy Horse was trapped in a telephone book
from an eastern city, the book thick
with names of those like himself displaced
in this displaced time & place.

He closed his eyes to let his mind focus,
then rang a random. After three rings,
"Hello?" someone said. Crazy Horse decided
to bust balls for misery's company in this future

as the whites' mid-century broke.
"What's the difference between a duck?"
Tasunke Witko asked. "A duck and what?"
the man replied. "Why is a mouse

when it spins?" Strange One continued.
The man dizzied as the Indian concocted
other metalogical puns & jokes:
two men in a shower, one drops his soap;

the first says, "You dropped your soap;"
the second replies, "No soap, radio.". . .
& the lonely human head rolling down a street
& singing, "I ain't got no body."

Such comedy evoked in you a vertigo
as though you'd lost being & meaning,
a man rowing in the middle of a lake
who stands & shouts, "Leave two milk!"

Repossession

Crazy Horse spotted Custer carrying two sacks of stars over his back.
Some were sticking through canvas & bursting with keen sacral light.
Bluecoat was bent over like a beggar with so much weight.

"Yo, dude, wassup?" Crazy Horse asked in his own lingo, pulling
an arrow from his quiver. "I claim these for my children, and theirs,"
said Custer. The arrow of Crazy Horse's thought,

& the arrow from his quiver—each was faster than the other:
despite summer, Crazy Horse stood over Custer like a hailstorm,
for his own daughter was dead, & he was out of time.

Crazy Horse & Custer in Cottonwood Spring

Almost didn't meet one was passing through
a tree from one side one from the other each
just wandering with nothing in mind this
big tree with so many rings to its spirit
that such non-beings travel inside it maybe
forever, but these two were close then closer
then recognized one another neither was taller
here or darker or dressed unlike the other or
bore with him language prefigured in memory
or opposition each was if anything only
earthcolor & eyelessness both east & west
for this duration the circular heartwood wavered
& conjoined them briefly into one while each
modulated the spectrum of the other but
it's impossible for us living to see very far
inside the afterlife of generative vision, which
continues. . . . They met, joined, moved on,
will sometimes meet again. The tree senses
what has entered & left it, & now each spring
fills its leaves with the sounds of feelings
that contain & reveal the future of everything.

Souls

Once, traversing
this land of souls together,
Crazy Horse & Custer shared a canoe
of white, shining stone through which
they could pass their hands, & feel water.
They flew over this water like an arrow,

each in front of the other, each behind the other
in this dimensionless place west
of the setting sun. Some words were spoken
about the irony of common destination
as their stone boat woke starfish
under the waveplains.

Elizabeth's Dream, 1890

Crazy Horse slept for a long time, all the time staring
   into her husband's eyes.
A light shone therein, a lone woman walked among
     a few pieces of furniture.
She smoothed her hands over beribboned breasts,
     gazed into a mirror
framed by innumerable small shells. Crazy Horse
     walked closer & seemed
to want to touch her, but at that moment she turned
     to see him there, & moaned.
Autie surfaced from his trance & reached for his pistol.
     The Indian could almost not
awaken before a bullet reached his heart, but did,
     as the woman died.

Deer Engine

When Crazy Horse
got close enough,
the deer's body
swaying on a rope
from a cottonwood limb
was a car engine
suspended from
a steel cable:
all life
had drained from it
into a rainbow pool

streak-mirroring it.
The Strange One
placed his ear
against the block
and closed his eyes.
He saw everywhere
the engine had been,
a couple hundred
thousand miles
across land
that seemed scoured

by bearclaws
filled with oil.
He spun the engine—
it rose tight
to its limb.
He watched it
spin downward,
then wound it again,
watched it spin
downward again.
Curious,

animals & birds
gathered around him
in his play.
He spent one lifetime
and then another
in a trance
of spinning,
himself becoming
a deer spinning
downward,
then upward. . . .

Desert Moths

Over the Vegas strip I see the clouds you saw,
Crazy Horse, black in a depth of blue so deep
you felt the world was eye—awake, asleep—

& saw you. Last evening, I & other gamblers
brushed through a thousand moths enraptured
by the pheromones of neon. At the huge cowboy,

one touched my lips & fell, then fluttered up again,
ecstatic in the midst of others. In this way
the dead still visit us as dust, as vision.

Postlude

Custer on horseback in his afterlife
enters a canyon where all is song. . . .

His shadow fuses into aura in the rock,
his horse drops its head to drink light. . . .

Now, truly, he feels himself welcome,
forgiven by the everything that sings. . . .

Leaves:

GHOST'S DANCE

The Hairy Child

Elizabeth had heard that a chief's daughter
bore the child of a white buffalo,
which animal appeared in the maiden's tent
walking on its hind feet, careful
as she lay there frightened, not
to injure her with its hoofs & horns. . . .
The hairy child grew in her, & was born. . . .

Walking Broadway one winter evening
fifty years after her husband's death,
for the first time in all that time Elizabeth
recalled this story from that other life.
She'd make proper use of it at her next lecture,
how the Indian maiden lay a still vessel
in the presence of such a god,

& conceived, & how the child was born
with white fur & the eyes of its mother.
But what had happened to this child?
Why could Elizabeth not remember? She,
of all people, burdened with history . . . Bells,
a sleigh whooshed past her through the snow.
What was it she needed to remember? . . .

Bugle

Elizabeth never saw the battlefield,
invited would not return, never,
but sees it now, this night,
kneels, afraid, perplexed at whether

denouement had occurred, or would.
All so vivid: blades of grass fiercer green
than she had ever known,
sharp-edged clouds moving slowly

in early-morning heat. "I must
not be here in case it has not happened,"
she tells herself, frantic
to wake, but her knees seem

rooted, she can only fall forward,
which she does, & lie prone,
her nose pressed into wildflowers,
as the charge sounds.

Flashbacks to Her Husband's Study

Atop his desk, a photograph of me in my bridal gown . . .
Over me, perched on antlers, a great white owl . . .

We often lounged about my husband's room twixt dusk and bed. . . .
Firelight reflected the glittering eyes of the animals' heads. . . .

Decades Later Elizabeth Remembers the Toads

The moss, though comfortable for bedding,
often held in its meshes the horned toad,
a harmless little mottled creature
with two tiny horns it turned from side to side

in the gravest, most knowing sort of way.
Officers mailed them home as curiosities.
Indifferent to air, at journey's end they jumped
out of the box, back in active service.

Elizabeth in New York Fifty Years Later

Sometimes, as I stand now at my window,
longing for the pack that whined with delight
or quarreled with jealousy for the best place near us,
my eyes follow each dog that passes in the street,
and follow its leash to its master. . . .

Elizabeth Remembers Tenting on the Plains

Always the terror of being late, that some day
hundreds of men would have to wait
because a woman had lost her hat pins.

Dakota A.D.

Libbie, packing to leave Fort Lincoln,
folds her husband's buckskin coat
atop camisoles in a steamer trunk,
traces her fingers along its lapels,

presses down fringes from elbows to wrists.
She will survive him fifty-seven years, dying
still in love with him to join him thereafter.
The Smithsonian coat exudes odors of deer.

Elizabeth in Gossamer Sleeplessness

We write the world as we read it.
It is not this or that thatness or thisness,
but consists for us of what, as we see, we say. . . .

Thus the moonlight in this room in a city of this
Twentieth Century, America: Autie is moonlight, breath
to breath, on my pillow. No reason

and never mind, I write him
back into the world, relume him, as we once were,
two as one, moon, you who were there.

Vellum Elm

Libbie lugged a bucket of ashes into her garden,
& dumped it, & forked leaves over the still-warm char
of unconsumed elm & graywhite powder.
Smoke sifted upward into late December air,

reminding her of something she has lately written
but cannot quite remember. Their lives on the plains
seem to smolder in her through leaves into the New Year,
seem illumined in her from ashes into the New Year.

Heaven

Libbie looked up & saw heaven filled with white tents,
the largest one aglow.
She blinked her eyes, then rubbed them, but the tents remained,
their canvas rippling
as though in waves of heat. This occurred the night before his death.
She wept because
she could not reach him, & went inside, saying nothing to anyone,
forgetting, until now,
as she leaves to join him, those tents pitched in heaven.

Our Sound & Souvenir

On this battlefield tonight, known only to us,
a sharp spring rain claws a single bone
to surface. From sluices in thatch, whiteness
rises, invisible, except to us.

A human bone, or the bone of a horse?
We read the light above this place,
this exact place, & now know: a soldier
stopped a bullet here, then arrows, & lost

his head, was stripped, his legs sledged;
then, the Indians gone, night descended,
the moon heat, the wolves. Eventual burial
by Benteen's men, unburial by animals, reburial

the next year, this leftover fragment of femur just
impatiently driven in like a knife blade. Now,
for the first time in more than a century,
it reaches surface. We look down

through where its marrow was.
We kneel, blow it clean,
take turns trying to see through it,
then place it between our lips to whistle.

Rounds

The frontispiece photograph in Mildred Fielder's
Sioux Indian Leaders shows six tipis & two men
blanketed against the cold. In front of them,

branches, but we can't see a fire. The caption:
"Crazy Horse lived in a village such as this,"
as he did, & didn't. He lives in the flow of ice,

in smokeless fire, in an otherlife of air & earth
within these hunched figures. Even when present
& forlorn in such a place as this,

he dwells in that elsewhere where time does
not make its seasonal rounds. Always
waits for him here . . . what? . . . That surety

of meaning: *Things come into me . . .*
the falling leaves . . . my people . . . the stars . . .
I watch them fall . . . they come into me. . . .

Camera Obscura

See into the photograph a dealer claims to be Crazy Horse
in a studio in front of a potted plant. . . .

Left hand's a fist, yes, Crazy Horse exists
in the black light within this hand,

otherwise & elsewhere than in the posed
bemused obdurate stare of this warrior, whoever.

History

In four sources we read the last words
of Crazy Horse, rendered as follows:

"Father, it is no use to depend upon me;
I am going to die."

"My father, you see I am hurt. Tell my people
they can hear my voice no longer."

"I am bad hurt. Tell the people it is no use
to depend on me any more now."

"Father, now is the time for me to die.
Tell our people I cannot help them any more."

MFA TQM

Appointed to three committees by the powers-that-be,
young Crazy Horse attended every meeting. . . . Not.
Enlodged alone, writing his witnessing, or smoke-
tranced with kindred spirits, the TA gave of himself until
exhausted, so got pissed when carpeted to account
by the smug tenured in their doctoral graves.
He tried, but couldn't pay attention, as accusations
enlightened him. The institution would dock his pay
if he was lucky; fire him, if luckier. Just in the nick,
reversing aversion to taking scalps, he woke
from this timewarp back to his wickiup, & rain.

Buffalo Commons: The Spiral

Long before either was born,
hairs in Crazy Horse's inner-ears

pricked to the scent of Custer's brain—
he knew where his people stood: at the magic

vanishing point of the rails, a dozen buffalo livers
for every spike & sleeper. . . .

                    Speaking of sleep,
I'm tired, & my theme spirals into the labyrinth
          of karma. . . .

If / when in the next time
we call Now, the Great Plains billows again
from wildflower dust,

the two will exchange places, one soul devolving,
the other hurtling upward to intersect & teach.

The Two Instincts

A cow buffalo's instinct to herd is almost overwhelming.
This one needed to migrate with her others, but

her calf lay bawling, something wrong with it, maybe
its back or a leg broken, I couldn't see for sure from that far,

but she licked its face, nudged her forefoot into its side, tried
to lift it with her nose, turned to leave with the departing herd,

grunted for it to follow, turned back, repeated these futilities
a dozen times as the others receded, until, frantic, trotting

toward them & back, toward & back, torn by the two instincts,
she bellowed, or moaned, & ran off, conflicted, in pain. . . .

Not long later, the young one struggled to its feet, stood tottering,
tottered forward, stopped, bleated to the empty hillside,

lay down again, dropped its head to the ground,
food for coyotes & buzzards . . .

but why assume anything while silver rays unreason the world
from so far away for so long

as they have from even before *homo sapiens* got here
from over the land bridge on foot &/or then

from easterly, cows & pigs tethered to wagons filled with guns
& furniture & children, to the windblown rainshadow

of the Rockies? . . . Whatever, I set myself to watch, & the herd
disappeared over the horizon of hills, when a single animal

came cleaving the duskscape & I thought, too large for a wolf,
I didn't know what to think, maybe a bear or other creature

omnipresent in all dreams under the moon, but then realized
the mother had returned all that way, she nuzzled

her baby again, urged it up, tossed her head toward the herd
to show the way, but her calf was dead, the two together

as darkness fell. I don't know for sure what happened next,
nor will. By morning, both mother & calf were gone.

This Creature

In my dream Crazy Horse reaches into his chest
to draw forth this contract, written on shell,
shell from a box turtle I remember.
He trusts it to me, questions in his laser eyes.
The turtle opens its trap-door

& peers up at its dreamer. My own hand
passes through my breastbone with the turtle.
I leave this creature there, alive, & wake,
a child again, having done, without thinking,
at least this once, the right thing.

Evolution

Repeated dream wherein a dog walks underwater
in graygreen dusklight, sniffing oozy bottom,
seeming in no hurry to surface to breathe.
It bumps lily-stems, the pads tremulous,
& tangles itself,

but slips loose again
all the way to dark. The moon thinks
nothing of this anachronistic pond creature,
backwards or forwards into history & future,
but shines through with its own gills & wavy fur.

Awakening

I dream I am crawling across the plains,
dragging three skulls on lengths of horsehair—
one tied to cuts in my left shoulder,
one to my right, the third to my spine. . . .

I am trying to lurch forward to break
thongs of muscle & bone, but the pain . . .
For a long time, I remain still. . . .
Six sockets burn in my back:

George Armstrong Custer, & one called *Tasunke Witko*
(one-whose-horse-is-enchanted), & you,
& himself dreamed by a skull-dragging dreamer who
does now, by grace, break free, & scar:

in the sky over this land a rift widens,
& all is sung in the earth colors of dawn.

Ghost's Dance: A Prophecy

I reach my bone hand into my own bleached ribcage,
withdraw a buffalo calf,
fist-sized, but perfect in every way—
fur, hump, hooves—& cream-white, her pupils

whiter than even her white irises.
I cannot not
realize what she is, or for how long
this being had marked time in her cage & refuge,

my breast. All will be well. I begin
to dance. Within me, now, prairie ramifies
with grasses & flowers,
sheets of lightning, the rumble of thunder.

Thereafter

The buffalo masticate the grass, juices
of the grass commingle with juices
of the tongue, the grass mushes into throats
& is swallowed, the grass builds fibre & blood,
the blood carries oxygen into the body,
the body of the herd increases & evolves
with rain & wolves across the spring prairie,
all herds-to-be-born present in the herd now,
all people-to-be-born present in the people now.

Poem

A buffalo wallow fills with snow,
snow drifting in cold wind & snow
from the sky. A wallow is not an eye
or brain to remember that other weather
when beasts rolled in relief. Now,
the land slows, widens, no one here,
no one yet to come for a thousand years,
snow & more snow, snow, prairie
tranced in whiteness, selfless crystals
of light & snow & the sound of wind
nothing is here to hear except for this.

Tarot

Crazy Horse shuffled & offered the deck to Custer
to cut. Light circled, stars im- & ex-
ploded in their chests in this vastness of afterworld
in which they were particles in an eye-mote
of the Great Mystery fulfilled. The deck
glittered transparently with hanged men, hermits,
lovers whose stories are still being played out
elsewhere. You suspect the rest: Custer cut,
the Other began laying cards out on Time's table,
the cosmos trembled like a newborn at the nipple
when mother caresses its head, & milk first flows.

Visitor

In the Plains Indian Museum in Wyoming,
I stared into the eyes of a stuffed buffalo,
first one & then the other. I did not see
in one Custer firing an Indian village;
I did not see in the other *Tasunke Witko*,
dismounted, firing into the forehead
of a soldier. In each brown & black glass eye,
I saw myself & exhibits around me, weapons
& costumes in cases in plains sunlight
flooding in from a skylight. The beast,
massive on its pedestal, did not countenance
history or sentiment but with man-made eyes
reflected me back past exhibits to exit.

December 29, 1890

The Sioux massacred
at Wounded Knee wear magic

white ghost shirts whose force fields
were not/can not be solved by white bullets.

The Rapture

In this place a buffalo's triangular head
becomes a mantis's—no, *is* a mantis's
at the same time, swivels on its neck-stem
360 degrees. Humped thorax shagged green,

the animal holds barbed front legs in the air,
rears back in threat, & prayer to the Great Mystery.
I cling to the fur of its furled wings, ready
for our next migration into death, this ecstasy.

The Closing

Golden sylphium & other summer growth-stems so resilient
that when buffalo trample the tall grass,
prairie springs up again to close behind them as they pass.

Curly Watches a Storyteller, 1850,

smooth ground with his hands,
make two marks in it with his right thumb,
two with his left, & a doublemark with both thumbs together,

then rub his hands together,
pass his right hand up his right leg to his waist,
touch his left hand

& pass his left hand up his left leg to his waist,
touch his right hand,
then do the same with his left & right hands

going up his sides to his breast, & then, with both hands,
touch the marks on the ground,
rub his hands together,

pass them all over his head, pass them all over his body,
& then begin.

Unbeknownst

Curly knew how easy it was for a buffalo
to grow horns, but he could not, no matter
how long he ran with his shoulders hunched over.
His friends laughed at him those days, of course,
but two nubs of light looked for & found his skull.

AFTERWORD

I was born in Brooklyn in 1940. My inchoate first memories are of noise, city streets, city smells, sidewalks, dark stairways, bricks, a bar & grill my father owned in Hollis, but when I was four or five, he went back to carpentry, his trade from the Old Country, and moved with his wife and sons about fifty miles east, first to Hauppauge & then to Nesconset. The latter name is from the Algonquin. It signifies "place of the second stopping" and the tribe of that place. For now, I have reached here. *Crazy Horse in Stillness* is dedicated to the Nesconsets.

Often when I was a boy, alone at ponds or in the woods of then largely-undeveloped Suffolk County on Long Island, I experienced states of reverie, felt the "impalpable sustenance of me from all things at all hours of the day" (as Walt Whitman says) that poets of primal consciousness sometimes embody in their poems. I of course had no language to describe these meditative states (& hadn't read any poetry), & feel only slightly more able to express them now, but they were times of mystical duration. Maybe because I had no special awareness that such experiences were extraordinary, I was not split from the natural world, observing it, as I usually am, as most of us this side of sainthood usually are, but was part of its being, its essence & spirit. Far from our house where my mother was fixing supper & worrying about money, far from the woodworking shop where my father was operating his ripsaw & worrying about money, far from them & at Lake Ronkonkoma or at ponds in the woods in a semi-trance, I believe I sometimes lived the life of present mind, if only for moments, that the Lakota boy, who was born a century before I was and who would later receive the name Crazy Horse, lived. I believe I am now sometimes still in touch with this life during my dreams, or during a few suddenly unselfconscious lightstruck seconds a day while going about my rational business, or during longer periods while reading or writing.

A lily pad trembled, a black head poked up in the stem-notch. I stared. The mud was warm to my ankles, the water warm to my genitals. I was completely *here*, fused with place & eternity. This, I think, was full consciousness in the truest sense, life lived without the qualifications & diminishments of habitual language. As the whites compressed and choked off his people, the Lakota boy must have felt that words were sacred. Words must sometimes have awed, sometimes scared him. He spoke less than others. He sought visions more often than others. To the end, he was faithful to what he knew. His collision with the consciousness of George Armstrong Custer—himself a man of complex sympathies— remains at the center of the experience we have inherited here in our place in time. *Crazy Horse in Stillness* seemed to come to me almost all-of-a-piece in just over two years. Sam Fathers in William Faulkner's "The Old People" advises young Ike to shoot fast & slow at once. Hopefully, this is what happened to me as this book came into being, & the reader will sometimes approach these timeless dream- or trance-states with me.

How to follow words & story to reach the sacred ground of our being beyond words & story? Sometimes, somehow, despite everything, by way of the fusion of rhythm-music-image-movement-thought, it can still happen; our world can still become meaningful for us in ways that might yet enable us not just to survive, but to live.

* * *

Many of these poems were set into motion by my reading during their writing. Sometimes, as when I used letters exchanged by the Custers, I stayed close to text (though I felt free to imagine myself part of an oral tradition, to adjust toward my own rhythms); sometimes, just an image or flash of a possible situation would lead me to a poem: I remember, for example, waking up in Las Vegas one morning, opening a book, seeing the phrase "white owl," & quickly drafting what became "Owl Winter." Most of these poems were written by way of their sounds and their flow/cut/plunge from line to line, & not by way, of course, of argument or idea.

Enough history is here—some of it in different versions—so that I haven't felt it necessary to include additional notes on places, persons and events; but I would like to mention certain sources (not repeating those from which I've taken epigraphs or those such as the Custers' books to which I refer in the poems themselves) that helped generate *Crazy Horse in Stillness*: George P. Belden's *The White Chief or Twelve Years Among the Wild Indians of the Plains* (1870—reprinted, with an introduction by Jack Matthews, in 1974); Evan S. Connell's *Son of the Morning Star: Custer and the Little Bighorn* (1984); Joe DeBarthe's *The Life and Adventures of Frank Grouard* (1894, new edition published in 1982); Richard Irving Dodge's *The Plains of North America and Their*

Inhabitants (1876, new edition published in 1989); Lawrence A. Frost's *General Custer's Libbie* (1976) and *The Custer Album* (1964); Francis Haines's *The Buffalo* (1970); Jamake Highwater's *The Language of Vision: Meditations on Myth and Metaphor* (1994); Eleanor H. Hinman's *Oglala Sources on the Life of Crazy Horse* (interviews from 1930 first published in Nebraska History Magazine in 1976); Jason Hook's *Crazy Horse: Sacred Warrior of the Sioux* (1989); George E. Hyde's *Red Cloud's Folk: A History of the Oglala Sioux Indians* (1936); Douglas C. Jones's *The Court-Martial of George Armstrong Custer* (a novel, 1976); D. A. Kinsley's *Custer: Favor the Bold* (new issue, 1992); William H. MacLeish's *The Day Before America* (1994); Thomas E. Mails's *Fools Crow* (1979); Anne Matthews' *Where the Buffalo Roam* (1992); Peter Matthiessen's *In the Spirit of Crazy Horse* (1983) and *Nine-Headed Dragon River: Zen Journals 1969–1982* (1985); Marguerite Merington's *The Custer Story: The Life and Intimate Letters of General George A. Custer and His Wife Elizabeth* (1950); Bill and Jan Moeller's *Crazy Horse: His Life, His Lands* (1987); Kathleen Norris's *Dakota: A Spiritual Geography* (1993); Red Fox's *The Memoirs of Chief Red Fox* (1971); Mari Sandoz's *Crazy Horse: The Strange Man of the Oglalas* (1942); Brian Swann's *Smoothing the Ground: Essays on Native American Oral Literature* (1983); Deborah Tall's *From Where We Stand: Recovering a Sense of Place* (1993); and James Welch's *Fools Crow* (a novel, 1986). I did not read Welch's reverberating *Killing Custer* (1994) until after I'd completed *Crazy Horse in Stillness*. Welch writes this of *Tasunke Witko*: "He did not braid his hair but wore it loose and long. He was a strange youth who would grow into a strange man. He never sacrificed before the medicine pole, an almost unheard-of thing for a Plains Indian. He never took part in sings and dances. He passed through the village without recognizing people. He stayed away from camp for long periods of time, even in winter. Throughout his life, Crazy Horse was as mysterious to his own people as he is to us today."

ACKNOWLEDGMENTS

Grateful acknowledgment is made to the editors of the following publications in which some of these poems first appeared:

American Poetry Review: "Crazy Horse Mnemonic," "The Tub," "Tongues";

Crazyhorse: "'Anticipatory Breach'";

The Long-Islander: "Bowl";

Long Island Quarterly: "The Bead," "N," "The Answer," "The Willow";

The Magazine: "Pollen";

North Atlantic Review: "Microcosm," "Epistemology," "One World," "Heat," "Tigers," "Leaves of Horse," "The Paper It's Written On," "X-Ray," "Thought," "Evening Heart Angel Ascension," "Timewarp," "Buffalo Dusk," "Ghost's Dance: A Prophecy," "Snow Maggots," "Karma," "Verdi," "Lakota Eye," "Her Husband in Moonlight";

Ontario Review: "Legend," "The Leatherstocking Tales," "The Streams," "After-Image";

The Southern Review: "The American Civil War";

TriQuarterly: "Before," "An Officer's Story," "Grasshopper Sperm," "Texas Gulliver Malaria," "Flame," "Placefulness," "Sorrow Village," "Mushroom River," "The Bear," "Breasts," "Repossession," "The Grave," "The Tooth," "Blood & Sage," "Scenarios," "Government Protection," "Duration," "The Steadying," "The Herd," "Visitor";

Witness: "The Calves," "Semicolon Gene Calves: Pool & Place Data," "Root Music," "Forces," "Wingdust," "Disk Text".

་ཀྵྀ

INDEX OF TITLES

ABOUT THE AUTHOR

One of the best-known poets of his generation, William Heyen was born in Brooklyn in 1940. A professor of English and Poet in Residence at State University of New York College Brockport, he has been a Senior Fulbright Lecturer in American Literature to Germany and has won prizes and fellowships from the National Endowment for the Arts, the John Simon Guggenheim Foundation, *Poetry* magazine, and the American Academy and Institute of Arts and Letters. Among his many books are *Long Island Light, Erika: Poems of the Holocaust, Pterodactyl Rose,* and *Ribbons: The Gulf War.* His *The Host: Selected Poems 1965–1990* appeared in 1994.

⤙⤚

BOA EDITIONS, LTD.
AMERICAN POETS CONTINUUM SERIES

Vol. 1   *The Führer Bunker: A Cycle of Poems in Progress*
W. D. Snodgrass

Vol. 2   *She*
M. L. Rosenthal

Vol. 3   *Living With Distance*
Ralph J. Mills, Jr.

Vol. 4   *Not Just Any Death*
Michael Waters

Vol. 5   *That Was Then: New and Selected Poems*
Isabella Gardner

Vol. 6   *Things That Happen Where There Aren't Any People*
William Stafford

Vol. 7   *The Bridge of Change: Poems 1974–1980*
John Logan

Vol. 8   *Signatures*
Joseph Stroud

Vol. 9   *People Live Here: Selected Poems 1949–1983*
Louis Simpson

Vol. 10   *Yin*
Carolyn Kizer

Vol. 11   *Duhamel: Ideas of Order in Little Canada*
Bill Tremblay

Vol. 12   *Seeing It Was So*
Anthony Piccione

Vol. 13   *Hyam Plutzik: The Collected Poems*

Vol. 14   *Good Woman: Poems and a Memoir 1969–1980*
Lucille Clifton

Vol. 15   *Next: New Poems*
Lucille Clifton

Vol. 16   *Roxa: Voices of the Culver Family*
William B. Patrick

Vol. 17   *John Logan: The Collected Poems*

Vol. 18   *Isabella Gardner: The Collected Poems*